GIULIANA TRANQUILINI
& SUSANA ARBEX

YOUR PERSONAL BRAND

BE AUTHENTIC & IMPROVE
YOUR PROFESSIONAL SKILLS USING THE FLY® METHOD

For information, please email contato@betafly.com.br

Copyright © 2024 Giuliana Tranquilini Hadade
Copyright © 2024 Susana Arbex
Copyright © 2024 BetaFly Brandmakers

First English Edition

ISBN 979-8-218-53759-3
Written by Giuliana Tranquilini Hadade & Susana Arbex
Translation Revisions Rodrigo Garcia
Cover art Antônio Belchior Neto
Designed Gabriel Uchima
Infographics Gustavo Comin
Typeset Vanessa Lima

Manufactured in the United States of America

Cataloging-in-Publication Data (CIP)
Angélica Ilacqua CRB-8/7057 - Librarian

T772y
    Tranquilini, Giuliana
      Your personal brand : be authentic & improve your profes-
sional skills using the fly® method / Giuliana Tranquilini, Susana Arbex. — São Paulo, SP : BetaFly Brandmakers, 2024.
    278 p. ; illus.

    Biography
    ISBN 979-8-218-53759-3
    Original title: Sua marca pessoal

    1. Branding (Marketing) 2. Personal brand 3. Success in busi-
ness I. Arbex, Susana. II. Title.

24-5322   CDD 658.82

Note
Much care and technique were employed in editing this book. However, there can be no assurance that it will be free of minor typing errors, printing issues, or even conceptual ambivalence. In any such case, we ask that the issue be notified to our customer service at the e-mail address contato@betafly.com.br

DEDICATION

Giulia, Lara and Malu, my daughters, you are my endless well of inspiration, you provoke me to be in constant movement, in search of my best for you.

My mother, Marlene, who taught me to never give up, to live with independence and faith. Your grit and determination inspires me.

To my dear in-laws, the parents life gifted me, Mrs. Jacqueline and Mr. Abdo, who are an example of unconditional love, openness and generosity.

My sisters Daniela, Roberta and Giovanna for bringing lightness, love and joy to my life and who I can always count on.

To Su, my friend and business partner, for the long nights and tireless exchanges.

Ale, my companion, my love, who is always walking hand in hand, pushing me to grow every day.

Without you all my journey would not be as fun and complete!

Giu

Ana Helena, Júlia, Juliana and Ana Carolina – my daughters, who bring me meaning, purpose and joy – my life is incredibly better because of you.

Nawal and Alberto, my parents, who taught me the value of truth, ethics and hard work.

Beto, my beloved brother and best friend in this life, who, alongside dear Liana, gifted me Gustavo, Mariana and Arthur; your five books that inspired me to write my first.

Giu, my friend and business partner, for everything we've done together and have yet to do.

Marcelo, my love, companion and supporter – our encounter changed my life forever and without you none of this would be possible.

To each and every one of you, grateful for the luck I have to have you on my journey.

Su

ACKNOWLEDGMENTS

To all of the clients that gave us the honor of your confidence throughout your professional journeys, your dreams and challenges, who we learn so much from and who help us become better people everyday.

A loving thank you to Alexandre Correia Alexandre Correia, Cecília Cavazani, Cintia Capasso, Eleonora Lobo Salles Leite, Eugênia del Vigna, Fátima Pessoa, Karina Lima, Maitê Leite, Mariana Lorenzon, Naná Feller and Thiago Coelho, who authorized us to share the contents of their Personal Brand, and in doing so help us inspire more people to believe in the power of a strong brand.

To the clients, partners and experts in our field who generously shared their testimonials about their experience with our FLY® Method, with statements that we never tire of reading – and being moved by.

Mr. Luiz Seabra, founder of Natura & Co, a company with solid values and a unique personality, with so much courage to challenge the status quo and actively promote positive changes in society.

Natura brought us together, strengthened the foundations of our professional trajectories, and because of it we met so many people who transformed our lives, especially our husbands and companions on this journey, Alexandre Hadade and Marcelo Araujo.

Christiane Pelajo and Daniela Cachich, for the friendship, for generously pushing us and being an inspiration to us and so many women #riseandraiseothers

Adriano Bravo from Petra Group, Dr. Fábio Saito and Caio Silva from Galderma and Silvane Castro from Seven, for believing and trusting our work.

To our friend Tonia Casarin, who generously shared her journey and introduced us to Dany Sakugawa, who knows everything about the publishing world and guided us on how to explore this path, and also introduced us to Dani Folloni, who, with her talent and never-ending patience, helped us give this book shape and structure.

Stephanie Carnieto and Júlia Brandáo, our angels of organization, for your hard work and for believing in BetaFly when it was just an idea.

Flávia Lima, our coach more than a partner, the BetaFly process would not be the same without her competence, dedication and sensitivity.

Marcus Sulzbacher and Antônio Belchior Neto, who with their celestial talent presented us with the most beautiful logo and cover we could ever dream of.

Regina Carvalho and her team at Arizona for the disposition, agility and final look to have the best color quality. Mr. Maurício and the Literare team, for believing in the project and accepting the challenge of publishing in record time.

To the Monk, our Master Ishwarananda, for inspiring the creation of the name BetaFly – not obvious at all – in a meditation retreat in the Pantanal.

PRESENTATION

Have you ever considered what professional recognition you don't have but feel you deserve? What type of success story do you want to tell about yourself? This is an opportunity to reflect on that and work towards making it a reality in your life. Throughout this reading, you will come across more reflections and questions that will lead you to find solutions and insights for strengthening your *Personal Brand* to make it more authentic and aligned with your desires.

You will get to know the stages of a process that gathers our experience of over 20 years in communication and corporate branding, tested and approved by hundreds of people so that you can also reflect on your brand and find your unique way to make your name remembered, recognized, chosen, and preferred. All of this without having to create a persona. Our methodology starts from deep self-awareness precisely because we believe that the best each person has to offer to the world comes from their essence, from their Identity.

After experiencing the Personal Branding journey, you will be able to tell your story authentically to achieve your goals and increase your value in the market. If this is what you need to have a more meaningful and rewarding professional journey, join us.

FOREWORD

Susana and Giuliana, the authors of this book, "discovered" themselves at Natura & CO, (a group of Avon, Aesop, The Body Shop and Natura brand) , a company I had the privilege of founding 53 years ago.

It brings me the greatest joy to think/feel about how our company sparked interactions of great intellectual, emotional, and affective richness. Many meaningful and transformative discoveries. Considering our whole network of relationships, a true legion of people were able to live the dynamics of life having discovered themselves, not only around the world of business but mobilized by causes, values, and principles, in addition to the joy of socializing.

By founding Natura, a seemingly impossible dream to many, I was beginning to manifest my personal brand. To the world and to myself. And it is from this "adventure" that this book deals with. The adventure of becoming. Nietzsche summarized it so well in his phrase inspired by Pindar, the Greek lyric poet: "Man, become who you are!" It is the adventure of discovering and expressing our potentialities. Some we couldn't sense, and others eventually repressed. The many "no's!" we heard in early childhood still echo within us, repressing us. Have we said yes to the life that inhabits us? Do we allow what called us to this life to manifest: vocation?

In this book, you will find the depths, expansions, and reflections these questions evoke. A book of action and adventures full of life, and life is movement. In a world that revolves around corporate brands and identities that make creators anonymous, the conceptual and practical development of how to reveal the singularity of each of us is of the utmost importance. The revelation will be that which only we can become: the expression of our personal brand. In the exercise of this authenticity, the possibility of finding the source of achievements and personal happiness resides: discovering the meaning, the reason for being, of our lives.

I hope this book expands consciousness and reveals potentialities, spreads transformations, and opens many paths.

Be happy about these discoveries!

Luiz Seabra,
Founder of Natura & Co

INTRODUCTION

Being Who We Are Meant to Be

What makes a brand recognized, remembered, and adored if not the fact that it puts all its power at the service of uplifting others?

We are leaving behind the era of personas and revealing the meaning of authenticity. The search for more truth in relationships gains strength, gradually replacing the construction of characters and presenting people to the world as they are. Revealing oneself genuinely is seeking support in the potentialities you want to show to the world. Not in the form of vanities, but through your proposed value. In this way, recognition and success become the consequence of our talents in action and in service of magnifying an individual, an audience, and society.

We believe that people strengthen their *Personal Brand* when they achieve a powerful combination: doing what they were born to do with their abilities and what they naturally excel at, while combining a purpose that brings them meaning to carry it out.

This is the authenticity that emerges from self-awareness and paves the way for us to choose. From our complexity as human beings and our numerous dimensions, we decide which ones will be revealed and with what intention. It is not about "sincerity," but instead, the confidence to present ourselves without masks to pursue our goals—without building unsustainable characters at the expense of our inner truth.

The price of not manifesting our essence is failing to exist in our most extraordinary power. Understanding this truth and with internal stabilization, we can establish genuine connections permeated by empathy and genuine interest. It is less about striving to be important and more about caring. Less about pursuing interests and more about being interested. Less about you and more about others.

It is in this flow that reputation is built and strengthened in the minds and hearts of the people with whom we interact, eventually becoming disseminators of our brand's message.

A brand that, much like a living thing, is in constant evolution by recounting and retelling our story. From this accepting, generous, and transparent perspective towards ourselves, we are shaping our own Identity every day.

Embracing our narrative is to exercise our true self.

It is a privilege that the human mind grants us, paving the way for recognition to come from who we are—and from everything we are meant to be. By embracing our narrative, we chart a life with more meaning and satisfaction, and we are recognized not only for what we do but for who we are. This leads to a greater sense of purpose and fulfillment, as well as more genuine connections with everyone around us.

Building *your Personal Brand* began long ago when you were born. What starts here is a journey of self-discovery, more conscious and that will promote the strengthening of your narrative. Ready?

1. This book was written in the first person plural. It synthesizes our learning, Giuliana and Susana, in over 20 years of working in Communication and Branding and working with Personal Brands. This content was co-constructed by the two of us but also has a bit of each of the people who trusted the FLY® Method to organize their narrative and who also left a bit of their brands with us. Therefore, in the text, we always refer to "we." When we are talking about a specific experience lived by one of the two authors, we will use "I, Giuliana..." or "I, Susana..."

2. The examples throughout the book are all based on real stories experienced by our clients. Complete case studies and specific content are referenced; names have been replaced for the other stories described.

WHAT OUR CLIENTS SAY

BetaFly played a very important role in my professional life, helping me deepen my self-knowledge, regain my self-confidence, and prepare for a new phase in life.

Adriana Leite
General Manager Central America Region - Colgate-Palmolive

Going through the process of building my Personal Brand with Susana and her team was transformative. It allowed me to see, overflow, and position myself in spaces consciously and completely, through tested techniques and methodologies, with empathy and competence. The FLY® Method transforms careers and lives.

Alessandra Benedito
Lawyer, University Professor, and Diversity Consultant

The process came at a very opportune time for me, as I was reviewing a business partnership and my work style. I wanted to change but didn't know how. The first significant benefit was identifying my strengths. Although these were not unknown to me, the process with Susana revealed my strengths and my argumentative capacity, giving me the confidence to follow a more autonomous path. One practical outcome was bringing a competitive edge to my positioning. I also awakened a dormant skill in the wellness market, which led me to become a mentor, gain new clients, and create new work opportunities.

Alexandra Jakob
Marketing, Retail, and Wellness Strategist, Founder - Allez Boutique de Estratégia

---

Between 2015 and 2020, I made an interesting career shift from the B2C universe to the B2B world, which I fell in love with. In my work, I transitioned from mass and statistical brand communication to a more direct and personal communication channel. At the same time, as digital networks matured, executives in Brazil began to understand the value of positioning themselves as ambassadors for their companies, brands, and legacies.

On a personal level, these shifts sparked a deep curiosity in me to understand more about the value and process of Personal Brand building. Honestly, I approached this investigation with skepticism rather than enthusiasm. I spoke with many professionals and practitioners, and that's how I met Susana, a brilliant and genuine person who captivated me and became the catalyst for a major transformation in me as a professional.

The process we went through went far beyond simply working on a Personal Brand and setting up a communication flow and thought leadership. Susana challenged me to reflect on my professional journey up to that point, refine ambitions, and map out future development paths. In the end, we translated all these learnings into a clear strategic positioning and a set of values and key messages to communicate this positioning to the market.

The process also encouraged me to express myself more, write better, and break down the barriers and biases we executives often have about using a personal, active voice and genuinely acting as ambassadors for our personal legacies and the companies we represent.

Alexandre Correa
CEO - Gerdau Graphene

The Personal Branding process with BetaFly was excellent for assessing changes in my professional positioning, discovering my strengths, and identifying the biggest challenges I need to face to be fully aligned with my new project or professional phase.

André Porto
Investor

The Personal Brand process was essential in boosting my career, taking me from 400 to 700 farms served. Through this crucial support, I was able to increase my visibility, convey my expertise, and build solid relationships, achieving surprising results and establishing my reputation as a reliable and specialized professional in my field.

Antônio Chaker
Agrobusiness Entrepreneur - Instituto Inttegra

I decided to work on my Personal Brand with Giu after participating in another project she led for the Personal Brand of one of the doctors in the clinic where I worked. Witnessing the challenges she posed and the transformations in the doctor inspired me to embark on the same journey. I reached out to BetaFly again when I decided to follow my dream of leaving the clinic and offering my expertise to other doctors. After the mentorship, this became a reality: today, I am a consultant specialized in people management at the largest medical consultancy in Brazil.

I absolutely loved it! Thank you so much, Giu, for everything we built together. It's incredible to see it all solidified, transitioning from 'gaseous' to 'solid.' Now, I see myself working with many doctors, fully connected to my purpose.

Carol Kitsis
Entrepreneur, People and Culture Professional for Clinic Management

---

My experience with BetaFly's Personal Branding mentorship was simply wonderful and enriching. From the very beginning, I felt I was in good hands and could fully trust the guidance I received. Susana is an expert in Personal Branding, helping me understand my identity better and build a strong, consistent brand. The BetaFly team is unbeatable—competent and dedicated—and they helped me achieve incredible results in a short period.

Carolina Papa Pagano
Wealth Manager

When I reached the 25-year mark of running my architecture office, I felt the need to 'refresh' my perspective on work and routines. I sought out BetaFly. Their personal branding work was immensely valuable in this process, leading me to a deep analysis of various personal and professional aspects. The feedback revealed surprising insights about how others perceived my work and myself. This diagnosis uncovered recurring blind spots and emphasized talents I often took for granted, allowing me to highlight them consciously. It was truly enlightening.

Carolina Rocco
Architect - Carolina Rocco Architecture

I consider the Personal Branding process with BetaFly one of the richest assessments I've ever done in my career. The combination of interviews with colleagues, self-assessments to identify dominant talents, and reflection on sabotaging behaviors provided essential insights to improve my current performance and refine my focus.

The main benefit of this process was understanding the gap between my 'actual self'—driven by my recent experiences as an achiever and influencer—and my 'ideal self,' which involves taking on strategic roles as an advisor. This clarity helped me revise my resume, articulate a new pitch for headhunters, and realign my LinkedIn posts with more strategic themes.

Carolina Rocha
Director of Retail and CPG - Microsoft

BetaFly's branding process felt like an inward journey to discover my place in the market and the world. It encouraged me to strengthen my natural talents and pinpoint areas for improvement. Giu made everything feel easy and enjoyable—three months of weekly meetings flew by! I already miss our sessions. Thank you so much; this process will undoubtedly be a milestone in my professional growth.

Dra. Catarina Carvalho
Dermatologist - Founder of Clínica Dra. Catarina Carvalho

I sought BetaFly's services to find a positioning that would encompass all the different facets within me: the construction businesswoman, the lawyer, the poet and writer, the woman, and the mother. Our challenge was to bring all these dimensions together harmoniously and powerfully into my Personal Brand.

Working with Susana was profound, methodical, and always strategically focused on achieving an authentic and memorable identity.

The result was sensational! Today, I can't even remember what it felt like to compartmentalize myself. The synergy from integrating all the 'Cecílias' was extremely powerful and, even better, it made me comfortable being my whole self. This made my communication flow more naturally and my positioning more organic, genuinely reflecting my essence in all areas of my life.

Cecília Cavazani
Co-CEO - Cavazani Construtora

Giu, the experience you provided for our clinic was truly incredible. It allowed us to better understand ourselves as individuals and recognize the importance of working together as a team. Secondly, you made us realize the importance of the Patient Journey. Although we already took good care of our patients, we saw that we could go even further in welcoming them and providing an even better experience. This became clearly evident after we implemented the suggestions you made.

For all this, I have so much to thank you for. Our next clinic will incorporate many of the lessons you taught me, and we'll continue this journey together.

Dra. Christine Guarnieri
Dermatologist - Founder of Centro de Dermatologia Christine Guarnieri

---

Susana guided me precisely through a well-structured methodology. With the right approach, I dived deep into my career trajectory, skills, and re-evaluated my plans for the future.

Additionally, I had the opportunity to gather feedback from my partners, leaders, subordinates, family, and friends regarding my strengths. It was incredibly enriching to use these insights as the foundation for building my Personal Brand.

As a result, I now have a clearer understanding of my professional profile and the brand I want to project to the world.

Cinthia Fajardo
General Manager - Playboy do Brasil

The BetaFly mentorship was a game-changer for me. It gave me profound insights into my vision, purpose, and values and helped me define the difference I want to make in the world and how I wish to leave my mark. It also made me realize my unique strengths, which I previously didn't fully value.

In summary, it helped me reframe my identity and improve my positioning with my stakeholders, which is now much clearer to me.

On another note, I made a LinkedIn post three hours ago, and it already has 4,900 views!

Since starting my LinkedIn activity after our mentorship, I've doubled my network.

Fernanda Sarreta
Vice President of Administration - IC Transportes

During the pandemic, in a period of deep self-reflection, I decided to embark on the Personal Branding process. Even with more than 20 years of experience across retail, consumer goods, and technology, I had several biases and fears about seeing and presenting myself as a brand.

The process led to several important realizations and shook me up in the best possible way. I learned that a coherent brand is one that communicates in alignment with its internal context, directed toward a goal or purpose. This journey gave me an awareness and structure that I probably wouldn't have achieved on my own.

Today, I feel confident in communicating authentically and apply this knowledge in both my personal life and professional work.

Flávia Villani
COO- Elo 7

As doctors, we tend to think we don't need help; we perform well academically and often don't stop to consider engaging in such a deep process. Giu was always very careful yet thought-provoking at the same time. This is something everyone should do at some point in their life—it serves as a great starting point.

A mutual friend of mine and Giu suggested I undergo this Personal Branding process specifically tailored for healthcare professionals. Honestly, I didn't know what to expect. Today, I am certain that this journey was the starting point for everything that lies ahead in my life and career. It gave me more confidence in making the decisions I needed to make.

Dr. Flávio Takaoka
Anesthesiologist, Program Supervisor of Anesthesia Residency - Hospital Albert Einstein, President of the Medical Council - Takaoka Anesthesia, Medical Board Member - Alice and Fin-X

The process led by BetaFly was extremely valuable in demystifying what Personal Branding means. Even as an introvert, I understood the importance of building a consistent and authentic brand. Without Susana's guidance, this wouldn't have been possible. It was serious work, with a solid methodology, yet incredibly human.

Irina Bullara
General Manager - RenovaBR

I sought out BetaFly to work on my professional image across the two markets I operate in as a dermatologist. Personal Branding is a rich process of professional self-awareness, where we identify the value attributes of my brand, its market positioning, and how I wish to communicate with the public.

Working with Giu, who has a specific method for healthcare professionals, was an essential foundation for defining clear and consistent communication strategies on the web, aligned with who I am and what I believe in. This material also provided valuable guidance for my marketing team and helped shape the next steps in my career. I highly recommend BetaFly to anyone wanting to build their brand with clarity, consistency, and coherence! Giu and Susana are exceptional!

Dra. Lilian Salvino
Dermatologist - Founder of Allier Clínica & HairMe

Going through the stages of the FLY® Method allowed me to tell my own story, and this process expanded my self-awareness. I've been working on self-awareness for a long time, and the process helped me amplify my strengths and shed light on development areas, effectively organizing my personal growth.

Luciana Domagala
Vice President of People and Sustainability - Ipiranga

Working with BetaFly came at a crucial career transition point, where we revisited my personal and professional journey and identified the main purposes for this new cycle.

The combination of sessions, content, and exercises was perfectly structured, giving me clarity and confidence to successfully navigate my career move. It was a rich, intense, and profound process that demanded dedication from both sides, leaving me with a method for diagnosing and addressing the challenges we encounter daily in the corporate environment.

Maitê Leite
Executive Vice President of Institutional Relations - Banco Santander

---

When I sought out BetaFly to build my Personal Brand, I believed that Giu's expertise in working with healthcare professionals would certainly be helpful for my professional challenges. However, we had so many excellent conversations, and Giu applied such practical methodologies throughout our journey, that today I can say I'm not just a better doctor but also a better person.

The stages of self-reflection, feedback, value design, and brand attributes led by Giu were all packaged in such meaningful meetings that I will deeply miss. She left me more prepared to grow, live, and soar. Thank you, Giuliana and the BetaFly team.

Dra. Marília Bronze
Dermatologist - Founder of Clínica Dra. Marília Bronze

Participating in this journey with you, Giu, made me believe more in myself and my dreams. You showed me my essence and how important it is for my life and my patients' lives.

One day, you told me that I should stay true to who I am—kind, cheerful, and full of laughter—and that I didn't need to change to connect with the new audience I wanted to reach. Being myself, as simple as it may sound, made all the difference in my life and career!

From starting my mornings with coffee accompanied by phrases of love, self-esteem, and care for each patient, to staying true to my essence every day, the journey was incredible. Your professionalism and sensitivity showed me what truly matters in achieving our dreams. I am a big fan!

> *'We are what we repeatedly do. Excellence, then,*
> *is not an act but a habit.'*
> **(Aristotle)**

And I strive for excellence every day by giving my patients love, care, and joy!

Dra. Milena Botelho
Dermatologist - Founder of Clínica Dra. Milena Botelho

The Personal Branding process should be mandatory at some point in everyone's life. Understanding how you present yourself, how you are perceived, and how you can view and position yourself—both personally and professionally—can truly guide or redefine many aspects of our work, no matter what it is.

I don't think I did it too late, but at the same time, I wish I had done it earlier. They say everything happens at the right time! Without a doubt, it gave me a new perspective, expanded my outlook, and provided the spark I needed to move forward, do things differently, or even continue doing the same things but with greater awareness. I loved participating in this journey of discovering who I have become and who I still can be!"

Samantha Dangot
Legal Director - IdeaZarvos!

___

Personal Branding should be mandatory for everyone, regardless of their title or position. Knowing who you are and how people perceive you (yes, it's not about what you are but about what they think you are) puts you in an advantageous position to ensure employability, success, and happiness.

Every process is unique, and mine served to consolidate what I already believed about myself. It helped me take ownership of my strengths and brought my plan B closer to my plan A. And what if I could live my plan B (even if adapted) together with plan A? What if I could bridge the gap between the two?

Thank you, Su, for your dedication, commitment, and care throughout this journey!

Talita Nakano
Head of Cloud Sales for Education LatAm _ Google

At 10,000 meters high, the seatbelt light comes on. Anyone who has experienced this knows the panic that sets in. However, deep down, you know that despite the turbulence tossing your internal organs around, you'll get through it—or, at best, nothing will happen.

Starting the Personal Branding process with BetaFly initially felt like light turbulence with no significant side effects. But as we delved deeper into the process, it became severe turbulence, shifting everything inside me.

It threw me off balance, giving me a new perspective to view myself differently. It was a time to pause, reflect, and rebuild in a new space and time.

Thank you, Susana, for this turbulence—our process was both affirming and invigorating.

Thiago Gonçalves
Latam Account Director - Hult EF Corporate Education

I express my formal gratitude to Susana Arbex de Araujo from BetaFly Brandmakers, whose solid work in #personalbranding and #personalreputation inspired me to achieve this status change, reshape patterns, and revisit pieces acquired throughout my journey—pieces that we cannot truly own until we ask ourselves: Who am I? How do I want to be perceived? What is my context? What makes me special and unique? And how can I translate all of that into a seamless communication strategy both online and offline?

Vanessa Sandrini
Retail Director - JHSF. Founder and Chairwoman of the Board - Instituto Mulheres do Varejo

---

I express my formal gratitude here to Susana Arbex de Araujo from BetaFly Brandmakers, whose solid work in #personalbranding and #personalreputation inspired me to make a status change, reshape patterns acquired over my journey, and leave behind certain pieces that I couldn't take ownership of.

It was a challenging yet enriching process. Susana's structured approach helped me redefine my narrative and develop a brand that truly reflects who I am today. This was not only about external visibility but also about aligning my professional essence with the perception others have of me, bringing coherence and consistency to my communication and positioning."

Zota Coelho
Creative Director - Zota Studio

TABLE OF CONTENT

Chapter 7:
Brand DNA 115

Chapter 8:
Positioning 161

Chapter 9:
Personal Brand Communication Strategy.... 185

Chapter 10:
Artificial Intelligence and
the Future of Personal Branding 245

Chapter 11:
Putting Your Personal Brand into Action 253

Chapter 12:
Live in Beta and Fly 261

CHAPTER 1

THE ERA OF
PROTAGONISM
IS WAITING FOR YOU

"**W**hat do they say about you when you're not in the room?" When the headhunter asked this question, Julia was intrigued. She didn't know what to answer. Days later, the question still echoed in her mind, and she sought us out. Julia had already gone through some feedback processes and self-discovery, but she realized she needed to look at herself through a new lens. She had felt the need to change how she managed her professional visibility for some time, but she didn't know exactly how.

The headhunter's question that made Julia want to break out of autopilot and redefine her role in the world is inspired by a reported quote attributed to Amazon founder Jeff Bezos: "Your brand is what people say about you when you're not in the room.". This statement gives many people the chills as they associate "talking behind someone's back" with something negative. However, saying something bad about us is just one of the possibilities. Sometimes, people speak well - very well - and contribute positively to affirming our role in the world. Whenever someone makes a positive reference to a person, indicating their work or recommending their service, they promote that individual's Personal Brand, even if they are absent. And that is very beneficial.

As the world becomes more interconnected, amplified by technology, the exchange of recommendations becomes more intense. Therefore, it becomes more relevant to understand how to position oneself and strengthen the attributes we wish to be remembered for. Connecting with this spirit of the times is essential to seize professional opportunities that align with your goals and purposes. Julia had already understood this but didn't know where to start from. "I can't identify my professional differentials, much less communicate them authentically," she told us.

Julia's doubts and difficulties are common to many people. This is because working on Personal Branding is very, very new. Few of us were educated or even encouraged to take control of our own narrative. Many people have spent most of their lives working and believing that by doing their tasks correctly, recognition would naturally follow.

Now, in a movement that may seem slow but continuous, we see an increasing empowerment of the individual in various dimensions. Those who lived through the 1980s to 1990s began to see consumers having more voice. In the 2000s, the individual became a media producer, having smartphones in their hands that allow them to take photos, record, write, and publish. This has led to an exponential rise of content creators who have the opportunity to gain notoriety, build authority, promote products and services, share their opinions, and even challenge major media corporations that were once the primary sources of information, content, trends, and opinions. Technology and social media have allowed people to amplify their voices.

Individuals have started to stand out, when in the past that would only happen with successful entrepreneurs. We have seen a growing appreciation for professional uniqueness at different levels within corporate structures. This movement has allowed people to gain more protagonism to the point of having a large reach like a major brand. This true revolution continues to grow.

There used to be a huge power imbalance between personal and corporate brands, regardless of the sector. While this asymmetry still exists to some extent, the gap is starting to narrow. In the past, it was almost a rule that when a person was part of a company, a clinic, an office, or any organization and left that job, they also left behind the company's reputation. This often causes a feeling of loss as many corporate brands add important attributes to personal brands, a certain type of status. Being under that umbrella increases a professional's market value. The issue is that many felt like they were small compared to a strong and robust corporate brand that validated and supported them. This still happens today, especially to those who spend many years within an organization and suddenly have to adapt to a new reality. The situation repeats itself with healthcare professionals who built their careers in large clinics and hospitals, in law firms with major offices, and in various other sectors. However, this reality is changing.

Today, even a person who chooses to remain in a robust institution– and feels an impact when leaving it– begins to realize: they have a voice and that this voice can resonate with other groups of people who identify with their message. They understand that there is value and strength in their authenticity and Personal Brand. This is an indication of the era of protagonism we are experiencing.

This is a time when we seek to understand who we are, what our potentials are, and how we can use them to serve a purpose. Being who we were born to be is a concept that encompasses endless possibilities. We are creating space for identities to not only reveal themselves more authentically but also to be valued for them. It is possible to find new ways of connecting with ourselves and perceive the value of our accomplishments without relying solely on having a corporate surname.

We see professionals moving more and more, transitioning between companies and brands and between work formats. One day, you may be an entrepreneur. The next day, you may sell your company and decide to work for someone else. At another moment, you may work on a project or act as a freelancer. With each change, you accumulate experiences and bring them from one place to another, enriching the story of your Personal Brand.

The exponential growth of startups is another sign of this phenomenon. Individuals empower themselves increasingly in a fluid, competitive, and interconnected world. This does not mean everyone must have a solo career or become an entrepreneur to take control of their Personal Brand. That's the interesting part. Social networks and the decentralization of media have brought an incredible opportunity for each individual to reveal their voice in any context, including the corporate world. In this new reality, people are taking control of their professional narratives.

We live in a unique opportunity in our history differentiating ourselves by who we truly are, without masks. Many people are gaining recognition for the transparent way they present themselves to the world. Julia is one of the many people who already perceive that we are in the era of protagonism. A time in which those who are able to stand out from the crowd gain more space, visibility, and recognition. And this is not just fascinating, it is an ocean of opportunities.

Personal Branding and the Future of Work

Alongside the decentralization of power from major brands and large companies, it has been common to hear that many jobs that will dominate the market in five or ten years have not yet been created. In the past decade, we have seen the emergence of several new jobs, especially those related to technological advancements and the increasing need for digital skills, such as artificial intelligence specialists, blockchain developers, cybersecurity professionals, augmented reality, and many others. But these advancements impact all professions. The two of us, for example, have worked for almost 20 years in Marketing and Communication. Two disciplines that were heavily influenced by experience, creativity, and sensitivity. Today, Marketing is a data-driven discipline. Just like in Medicine or Law, it is difficult to determine which areas of work will be immune to this transformation, but few are likely to escape some form of change. Knowing this can generate a certain anguish because it brings a sense of powerlessness. After all, what should be done with this information? How can one prepare today for a scenario that no one knows what will be like?

If this perspective is so uncertain, we can find solace in knowing that just as you do not know what the jobs of the future will be, no one else knows either. As technology continues to evolve, professionals need to relearn and review their knowledge to improve themselves while growing and keeping up with the market.

One way to prepare for this uncertain future is by working on your Personal Brand and making your capabilities clear. We always say that taking care of your Personal Brand in a rapidly evolving moment is a matter of survival. When a job that did not exist before arises, it is impossible to ask as a prerequisite of the people applying for experience or some previous training. What is usually sought are parallel or connected activities to those already done. It is a form of analogy, and working on your Personal Brand brings clarity to this.

If something you have already practiced in the past is similar, the recruiter/employer's thought process might be: "Well, since this person has gone through this experience or has this skill/ talent, they will be able to deal with this challenge." That is the logic: professionals will seek new positions based on what they are recognized for doing well. This applies to jobs as well as projects or ventures. In the innovation environment, this is a constant. Building your Personal Brand is a way to showcase your abilities. Additionally, although automation and artificial intelligence are replacing many functions, human skills such as leadership, creativity, and the ability to adapt to changes are likely to be highly valued. We often hear in Silicon Valley: "The more technological the world becomes, the more human we need to be." Having clarity about your human skills is part of the Personal Branding journey. By developing a strong Personal Brand, professionals can protect themselves against the "automation of work" and stand out in the highly competitive market with their human differential, in other words, their set of talents and what makes them unique individuals.

This happened to radiologist Patrícia who decided to open her own practice after acquiring state-of-the-art equipment for an ultrasound. With 14 years of experience and a partner in a popular radiography clinic, she knew that professionals in this field would be the first to be impacted and replaced by technology. In this scenario, she understood the importance of not only using the newly available technology to her advantage but, above all, working on her Personal Brand to highlight her differentiators and human skills to generate connections with patients and referring physicians. By doing so, she increased her clinic's results by 30%.

As individuals feel the need to organize the narrative about themselves, we are starting to see a growing movement in the search for understanding how we can become protagonists of our own story. Finding the answers to this search is possible once you start strategically working on your Personal Brand.

The word is confidence.

I left the process feeling much more confident in my position and my abilities than when I started.

BetaFly's methodology is highly interactive and places us in a space of provocative reflection. We are given tasks that require us to pause and look within ourselves. Often, this is uncomfortable, but it seems essential for the process. Working on Personal Branding is important because it makes us reflect on who we were, understand the skills we have, and identify the ones we don't. It helps us acknowledge what we've achieved in our professional lives and where we still want to go — and, sometimes, where we don't want to go. This methodology encourages that kind of reflection and analysis.

The tasks felt challenging because they were simple yet deeply meaningful questions. However, answering them was very interesting, as it allowed me to revisit my professional journey, my achievements, and things I had overlooked or failed to value. It was a truly enriching experience!

This process gave me strength, confidence, and direction toward where I want to go, leveraging my strengths.

The meetings with you, Su, were incredibly valuable. After every meeting, I felt like we were taking a leap forward, learning, and gaining new insights.

The interview feedback, the user-friendly platform, and the unique questions—different from what people are used to—really stood out to me. I truly enjoyed the methodology. It was a moment to pause and reflect on my life, and the process brought closure.

Rosane Menezes Lohbauer,
Founder and Managing Partner - SouzaOkawa Advogados

CHAPTER 2

WHAT HAVE
YOU NOT SHOWN
TO THE WORLD YET?

For some, the era of protagonism empowers or even liberates. For others, it brings more learning and evolution. However, the fact that all of this is possible and good does not mean it is easy for everyone. Some people will be more inclined to take on leadership and adapt to the new reality. For others, the feeling may be one of longing for when the organizational surname defined and simplified their role in the world - and the range of possibilities that open up beyond life in companies can cause a certain discomfort.

Many experienced professionals in various markets have been experiencing this reality. And they still begrudge a discomforting position in the audience watching people with much less to offer to the world already using their voice and resonating their message. When we come across those who dare and show up more, even though they may seem to have less mastery or depth on a particular subject, the need to increase our visibility starts to scream in bold and capital letters. This brings us exactly to one of the biggest complaints we hear from our clients: "Less competent people have more visibility than I do."

We see an explosion of "ordinary" people projecting themselves. They become an inspiration for many and are considered true models of success. The apparent perfection of these personalities– some perfect even in imperfection– only adds to the anguish of mere mortals: Can one stand out in a market filled with celebrity professionals? That was what Julia wondered as she realized that despite having built a consolidated and consistent professional trajectory, she did not have the recognition she deserved. She felt undervalued. At the same time, she could not have a clear view of her importance and place in the world, judging herself to be just a cog in a wheel without a clear purpose.

It is common to see in our daily lives people full of virtues, qualities, knowledge, and a hidden power failing to deliver their best to the world. This oscillating duality between knowing oneself to be capable and doubting one's own ability leads many people to hesitate when fostering their Personal Brands. The questions that consistently echo internally are:

- *"Will I make a fool of myself by exposing myself?"*
- *"After going through so many professional experiences, how do I organize my narrative?"*
- *"How do I look at my own story and extract meaning from it?"*
- *"What slice of my story makes the most sense to share at this point in life?"*

These questions demonstrate a necessity individuals have developed to be able to look at their own trajectories from a perspective that allows them to connect their lessons learned in an interesting way and that demonstrates how everything a person has experienced makes them valuable.

Take the case of Helena, who always preferred to work behind the scenes and avoided positioning herself as a leader. In her view, her role as a CEO was to be a facilitator who could support her team members so they could shine. Therefore, she invested energy in empowering her team. However, even though she did not feel the need to be in the spotlight, there was something she wanted to show about herself to the world. She did not know how to put herself in the spotlight while respecting her essence and values. For Helena, being humble was the reason that created a barrier between her and everything she could show about herself. After all, she did not consider it consistent with being humble and put herself in the spotlight. This became clear when she approached us with a poignant question: "What is the brand of someone who is both secure and humble, at the same time?"

As Helena retold her own story from a more generous perspective, she began to realize that sharing her experiences with the world was not simply bragging about achievements. After we conducted her assessment, it became clear that we were dealing with an extremely strong person. In her case, there was much to share, which would also be generosity towards other people. How many inspiring experiences were left untold? How many helpful learnings were not being shared? Taking ownership of the power and impact of her stories, Helena became more comfortable with the idea of being in the spotlight. At the end of our process, we were thrilled to see her literally on the stage of Sala São Paulo presenting an event for 1400 people, with the confidence of someone who knew exactly why she was there and that occupying that space was as genuine as it was deserved. From then on, there was a succession of events, lives, and interviews. Helena is an inspiring woman and staying in the shadows would be depriving the world of knowing that a leader can be both extremely strong and humble. That strength becomes more impactful because it is wrapped in kindness.

Another example is Eduardo, who had an internal and daily battle with the difficulty of networking. He felt a blockage that prevented him from approaching people and struggled to make contact first. This caused him to miss out on good opportunities in his field. His fear of being intrusive also led him to put some projects on hold. This was frustrating for him because he knew he was missing the chance to live more in alignment with his essence and to contribute to the world in a more effective and impactful way.

The need to work on Personal Branding can also arise when it is time to say goodbye to the corporate surname but taking credibility and authority already built within the companies with you. This was the case for Fernando, a lawyer who started his career at a renowned firm. With 20 years of experience, he built a solid trajectory and has gained a lot of visibility in his area. He realized it was time to work on his name and enhance his accumulated learning. The plan was to set up his own practice and operate more in line with his style, beliefs, and methods of action. Even though he knew his worth, he couldn't create his visibility alone. This is a common pain for many first-time entrepreneurs-- and even for those who already have an established business. In addition to this, some other complaints and requests come from business owners and independent professionals, such as:

- *"The fluctuation of the number of projects and not having an office size compatible with my resume bothers me."*

- *"I want to be able to choose more projects and clients and have to pursue them less."*

- *"I want my company to be recognized in the market as trustworthy, transparent, and with technical quality, meeting the client's needs promptly."*

- *"I feel there is confusion between my name and the name of my company. I have been working in the same place for so long that I don't know if people know where the organization ends and where I begin."*

In these cases, the values of Personal Branding shift from the individual to the legal entity. Therefore, the process that begins with self-awareness can be expanded to a purpose beyond individual projection. It helps you bring out into the world what is still stored inside you in an even broader way, making the foundation of your company's values.

Your Personal Brand already exists

Like Julia, Helena, Fernando, and Eduardo, you may also have something special to show the world. Waiting for the perfect moment to start this work is a big mistake. This is because there is no such thing as "not being in the world". Your Personal Brand already exists - it has been built as you have been acting.

People tend to draw conclusions and form mental images in order to create their own definition of who we are. They continue to label us based on the impact we make on them, whether we like it or not. Therefore, we are always creating an effect that builds upon the perception others have of us. There's no escaping from that.

If you are less active and visible in the world than you would like, you are more likely to not be perceived for what you consider most relevant: your true identity. So, we invite you to step out of the distressing mode and start organizing your narrative by choosing what you want to highlight about yourself, your journey, your story, and your talents. Taking control of your story and starting to be remembered for what you desire and value shows the world the most authentic version of yourself.

Dear Giuliana Tranquilini,

I would like to express my sincere gratitude for the personal branding process we undertook together about two years ago. Throughout this time, you have helped me explore and embrace my fascination with ideas, develop greater self-confidence, and respect who I am.

For me, an idea is much more than just a concept. It is a powerful connection that delves into the essence of events and phenomena. Developing a simple idea that explains complex events is fascinating. The pleasure of finding connections between seemingly unrelated phenomena motivates me and, without a doubt, makes communication with my patients and peers much easier.

With the help of the BetaFly team, I was able to see challenges from a new perspective, using the ideas and processes you introduced during the development of my Personal Brand. You encouraged me to review, analyze, look from new angles, and question preexisting assumptions. This approach allowed me to discover innovative possibilities, clarify my vision, and be more authentic. Walking this journey with a defined purpose is a fundamental step toward career growth.

Once again, thank you, Giuliana Tranquilini, and the entire BetaFly team, for all your support and guidance throughout our Personal Branding development process.

Warm regards,

Dr. Fábio Saito,
Plastic Surgeon - Founder of Fábio Saito Plastic Surgery

CHAPTER 3

WHAT IS PREVENTING
YOU FROM WORKING ON
YOUR PERSONAL BRAND

We see many competent people struggling to work on their Personal Brand. Some even feel blocked, as if it's not meant for them. When we investigate the reasons holding them back, some common justifications arise. We listed these common ones below, and if you identify with any, know that you are not alone—there are ways to overcome these obstacles.

"I don't know how to sell myself"

One of the most common arguments from clients who still need to start working on their Personal Brand is this: "I feel like this is important, but you see: I hate selling myself. I don't like exposing myself." Some believe that the best strategy to "be bought" involves impressing others by extensively discussing their qualities. Those who don't feel comfortable doing that think they won't be able to strengthen their Personal Brand.

This happened to Marcos, who always felt uncomfortable with his boss's feedback suggesting that he needed to sell himself more. He disagreed and hesitated, even though the company strongly encouraged executives to showcase their work to higher ups. The result was that many innovative projects he led only gained visibility about three years later when they had become more common in the market.

If you avoid showcasing your accomplishments because you don't want to borrow someone's ear to boast about victories and list your attributes, that's okay. Let's be honest, that kind of behavior can be really unpleasant. And it can also come off as arrogant. However, we also know that many call this "selling yourself." Unfortunately, this idea has also been absorbed by the market and confuses everyone.

Someone who is "selling themselves," or enjoys "selling themselves," isn't necessarily concerned with serving others. A person who only "sells themselves" uses others as a tool or means to talk about their favorite subject: themselves. This logic is geared towards self-promotion and tends to be quite tiresome for its victims.

If your intention in reading this book is to learn how to "sell yourself", we need to warn you that you may be disappointed. We, Giuliana and Susana, don't know how to do it nor do we want to learn or teach it. We don't believe that this approach generates good long-term results. That's because we don't see people as products on a shelf. People are not for sale. People are in service. Someone only becomes truly relevant when they can offer something that serves others – not when the central focus is on themselves. Personal branding is not about selling, it's about what you can do to make someone else's existence, career, and life better. For example, when a person dedicates their time to attending a lecture, of course they are drawn by the topic and the speaker. But at the end of the day, they expect to hear something that makes a difference: an experience, a learning, an inspiration. They want to leave the lecture with something that will make their lives better.

So, it's okay not to want to "sell yourself". This is not necessary to work on your Personal Brand. Instead of thinking about selling, we suggest that you start reflecting on the lessons you have learned throughout your history and how they can impact others.

It's an exercise in empathy. By shifting the focus from yourself to others, you share parts of your journey that are relevant to the goals of other people. From there, you don't need to sell yourself anymore, because you become relevant and allow others to tell your story for you. People do recognize a job well done. But it's your responsibility to "help others help you". In other words, your job is to show others the value you bring to the table. This strengthens your Personal Brand tremendously.

"I'm afraid of people's judgment"

Juliana, an executive who built an international career in a major oil company, was recognized for her success in implementing systems and managing multicultural teams. She knew she had valuable experiences to share. Sometimes, she would even write a social media post, but whenit came to publishing it, she would hesitate. It took her weeks, sometimes even months, to gather the courage to post. Most of the time, the content never made it out of the draft stage because Juliana was afraid of how her story would be interpreted by the public. She didn't want to "come off as someone trying to show off", as she confided. Along with this justification, there are many other reasons that the human mind creates to protect itself from what it believes will lead to being ridiculed or judged.

The fear of outside criticism is incredibly common. Juliana couldn't see any other possibility besides embarrassment. She couldn't see that her stories could be appreciated by people. She also failed to realize that her Personal Brand had a strong attribute of being cosmopolitan due to her global experiences, which added an extra charm to everything she discussed. At that moment, she couldn't see that instead of being ridiculed, she could be seen as relevant and interesting.

The fear of judgment often prevents many people from using social media, as well as other forms of exposure, whether in person or online. But this fear shouldn't paralyze you. Our experience shows that this fear diminishes when there is clarity about the intention behind each piece of content being shared. Therefore, the crucial questions to answer are: "Who is this message for?" and "What do I hope to achieve with this message?" If you are clear about who you are and the value you offer your audience, you shield yourself from external judgment and stay true to your purpose of serving others.

Working on your Personal Brand helps define which aspects of your life are relevant to your audience. When you understand that it's not about you, but about serving others, the fear of your self-esteem and reputation being affected disappears. This is because you anchor yourself in your mission and understand that the primary goal is to contribute to others.

"I need to prepare a little more"

Some people believe they are never ready to start increasing their visibility. They want to work on their Personal Brand but set a series of conditions for themselves to begin. They need to take another course, gain more experience, be in a job that aligns more with their interests, and have a certain number of clients and so on. The problem is that time passes, and you know what happens? They continue to believe they are not ready. In parallel, the list of credentials they feel necessary to embark on their Personal Branding journey only grows longer with criteria they set themselves.

Does this story resonate with you? Perhaps you are also a victim of imposter syndrome. This feeling haunts us internally by telling us we are a fraud, or we got to where we are by luck or because someone helped us. This feeling creates a barrier making us believe we are not good enough to put ourselves out into the world. A symptom of the impostor syndrome is being certain that at any moment, someone will discover we are not as competent as we believe ourselves to be. Another symptom is believing our resume defines us. Many people cling to the fact that they don't have a trajectory considered one hundred percent "top-notch" because they think only prestigious colleges and positions in renowned companies qualify them to occupy certain roles and gain visibility. This was the case for Felipe, a successful entrepreneur who built an innovative business from scratch, reached a very robust level, with a presence in multiple countries and a significant revenue stream. Despite his accomplishments, he felt uncomfortable with his own narrative for two reasons: (1) he started working at a young age and didn't have the opportunity to attend a prestigious college, and (2) his first entrepreneurial attempt was not successful.

Consequently, his focus on his Personal Branding process was less about creating an external narrative and more about organizing the narrative for himself. He didn't realize that the aspects he considered weak were, instead, incredibly appealing for building a strong Personal Brand. His early career struggles would serve as inspiration for many people going through similar situations. And his initial business failure set him apart in a very positive way, especially in innovative environments like Silicon Valley. The key was to make peace with his internal narrative as soon as possible and become more comfortable sharing his extremely inspiring story.

Feeling inadequate or not competent enough to expose yourself can have many origins, such as low self-esteem. If you identify with this profile, it's worth investigating the cause with the help of a specialized professional. Alongside this, you can begin working on your Personal Brand. Our experience suggests that most likely, you are not as unprepared as you imagine. We all have something to offer to those who are interested, in need, and understand our value.

Interestingly, those who are overly concerned about being fully prepared are often more than ready. They should start sharing their knowledge, showcasing their experience, and making their presence known. However, they feel so responsible for what they do and deliver to their audience that they never feel quite comfortable enough to show themselves. On the other hand, those who have a bolder attitude may not have this concern and simply move forward. Impostor syndrome is not part of their lives. And if fear were to strike, they proceed in spite of it.

Of course, continuous learning should be a life attitude. The concept of being a lifelong learner is here to stay. In the evolving pace of life, continuous improvement is essential. It's precisely for this reason that we can't believe we will ever be a hundred percent prepared at any given time. No one is. The important thing is to understand that you don't need to know everything to attract people's attention to your Personal Brand. You can set it in motion with what you already have. The day to start is always today.

"I'm an introverted person"

A very common myth is that working on your Personal Brand is linked to the necessity of being outgoing. Extroverts may have an easier time communicating, but someone who loves to be the center of attention is not mandatory to develop your Personal Brand. For those with a more reserved profile, there are ways to work on your brand without having to become someone else. In fact, the majority of our clients are introverted.

Susan Cain, author of the bestseller *Quiet: The Power of Introverts in a World That Can't Stop Talking*, says that society accommodates a very limited number of personality styles. There is a belief that to be successful, we have to be bold. To be happy, we have to be sociable. She refers to this as the Extroversion Ideal, which makes us admire people who love to be in the spotlight. According to this ideal, introversion with its related traits like sensitivity, seriousness, and shyness, is considered an inferior personality trait – which is a misconception. More reserved individuals are generally more depth-oriented in their topics, meaning they delve deeper and, therefore, have a wealth of knowledge to offer the world. That is how you can approach your Personal Brand with an introverted personality: fewer connections, but deeper ones.

"I don't have a relevant differentiator as a professional"

If you think nobody will be interested in your content, you're not alone. We often hear this as a justification for not working on Personal Branding. Typically, this kind of conclusion comes from individuals whose journeys are usually filled with achievements, results, and overcoming obstacles. When we take a closer look at their stories and experiences, we often uncover fantastic episodes worthy of a TV series. It's intriguing how individuals with such rich experiences can conclude that they have absolutely nothing extraordinary to share. Isadora had this view of herself, and that's why she came to us. As a facilitator in innovation processes, she is a very creative person. She has the ability to look at complex situations and propose something simple to help people organize themselves. Because of this, she had already developed some unique methodologies for facilitating groups and innovation processes and applied them with excellent results. She wanted to understand how she could combine all her experiences and skills to create something unique and valuable for people. Her goal was to create a value proposition as a facilitator and gain a clearer understanding of the importance of her expertise to her audiences, thus building authority in a topic she genuinely mastered. She achieved this by creating a thread for her message, which is a concept we will discuss later. Additionally, she developed a B2B business model to sell her expertise in creating methodologies.

In other cases, episodes of professional setbacks can lead a person to wrongly conclude that they are no longer good enough to occupy the position they desire. For example, this can happen after a sudden dismissal. When self-esteem is deeply shaken, it becomes difficult to see promising prospects. Some people overcome this phase while others struggle to turn the page, especially when re-employment takes a while.

Insecurity about one's ability can also be a feeling that intensifies gradually as we become more focused on execution and drift away from our essence and purpose. This process becomes more painful when the mind produces a flood of self-criticism. We have clients who believe so much in the negative evaluation they make of themselves that they struggle to see themselves as others see them. They go as far as receiving many compliments but feel as if they don't apply to them. In these cases, a structured Personal Branding process greatly helps reconnect with their own truth, guiding the person step by step to rediscover their potential, see their value, and own it.

"People with my seniority don't need to"

Maturity is inevitable but staying in constant motion while seeking evolution is an attitude. We consider the idea that having a certain age, "X" years of experience, or reaching a certain level of seniority in your career is a reason not to work on your Personal Brand to be very limiting. We see that it is very limiting to think that being of a certain age, having "X" amount of years of experience, or a certain level of seniority in your career is a good enough reason to not work on your Personal Brand. On the contrary, we see only benefits. People are not like product brands that require many processes to change direction. Because being human involves sleeping and waking up each day a little different from the day before. We are continually developing. Do you know someone who has reached the pinnacle of what they could achieve? Or who is ready, finished, and has absolutely nothing left to learn? We are fond of a phrase that says, "Today better than yesterday, tomorrow better than today," inspired by the Japanese Kaizen methodology of continuous improvement.

An example that age doesn't stop anyone from working on their Personal Brand is our client Marcelo, a 72-year-old anesthesiologist. He came to us because, during the pandemic, he was forced to leave the operating room. Dr. Marcelo had no intention of retiring at that time but was considered a high risk due to his age. The situation accelerated his plans, and he needed to find a new way to stay active and put his mark to use in a different format than in the operating room.

With no idea of what the new endeavor would be, he came to us for help in the process. Dr. Marcelo is an active, curious, restless, innovative, ahead-of-his-time doctor, and also a passionate adventure sports enthusiast. In his professional history, he has accomplishments such as being one of the first Brazilian doctors to perform a liver transplant surgery.

His journey was a beautiful and surprising process! Dr. Marcelo discovered new aspects of himself to chart a new path with his entrepreneurial version. His goal became clearer throughout the journey: to develop a program to empower doctors to prepare for the "new future" of medicine. In this process, he expanded his networking, getting closer to young entrepreneurial doctors who created startups and participated in a hackathon, a programming marathon that brings together programmers, designers, and other professionals involved in developing digital software and hardware. Additionally, he connected with organizations and groups of doctors to give lectures, speeches, and took on advisory roles in some startups. During his journey, he organized his narrative, embracing his talents as an entrepreneur. All of this contributed to strengthening his Personal Brand and the legacy he will leave in the market.

We live in constant rebranding. Every day, we add new layers to our story. The brain's neuroplasticity is evidence that we can be in continuous evolution. In his book *Soft-Wired: How the New Science of Brain Plasticity Can Change Your Life*, Dr. Michael Merzenich identifies 10 principles of neuroplasticity, and two of them support the importance of perseverance: the more you try and the more motivated and alert you are, the greater the change in your brain. The more focused your brain is the further you will go. Therefore, have willpower. And remember, initial changes are temporary. For a change to become permanent, your brain needs to judge whether that action truly brings you any advantage and then make that pattern permanent. So, persist!

In 2022, I, Susana, experienced one of the most remarkable moments of my life: witnessing my mother, Nawal, defending a master's thesis. At 72 years old! A few weeks later, it was my turn to graduate as a counselor at 52 years old, from Saint Paul Business School, ABP-W Program. When I decided to make a single post sharing these two achievements, I never imagined the amount of praise we would receive for our passion for learning, in a significant engagement for my network. What I did to honor my mother ended up highlighting how relevant it is to talk about lifelong learning, especially considering the perspectives of increased longevity.

For some things, there may be a more appropriate age. But for many others, the supposed limitations are myths. How do you differentiate one from the other? Testing and working on your Personal Brand will certainly help you find those answers.

"I'm not a celebrity"

You may not have the intention of becoming a famous person and, therefore, have not yet started working on your Personal Brand. But it's not only those who aspire to be celebrities who benefit from such a process. In fact, you don't need to desire fame to prioritize this effort in your career!

People in traditional occupations can —and should —share their experiences and values. Having a Personal Brand doesn't necessarily mean stepping onto a stage or having millions of followers. It's about being visible to your target audience benefitting from what you do, know, and say. It's not about gaining popularity, but rather notability. It's a kind of selective fame in the environment where you make a difference. It's about keeping your name in the minds of those in your professional circles, being remembered and invited to projects, gaining recognition, and being valued.

Carolina had a brilliant career and was already a CEO when she came to us. For a long time, she didn't focus on showcasing her achievements. Being someone who doesn't seek the spotlight, she maintained a discreet style. The need to strengthen her Personal Brand arose when she realized that, despite being known in her field and holding a senior professional position, she lacked visibility in the market corresponding to her trajectory. This was not favorable to her career plan, which involved rebalancing her schedule, and moving away from operational tasks to more inspirational endeavors. This was not an easy task. Some tough realizations needed to sink in, such as assuming the responsibility to become an inspiration as she desired and becoming more visible to the world. Overcoming this hurdle, Carolina took center stage by highlighting her Personal Brand in topics associated with influence and a new opportunity arose, fully aligned with her expectations.

"I don't need to work on my brand. If I do my job well, I'll be valued"

Many people think it's silly to consider Personal Branding because they grew up hearing advice like, "Stay quiet, do your job well, and recognition will come." There's a belief that a good professional doesn't need to worry about standing out, as their work will be enough to set them apart. This stems from the expectation people hold that life is fair: bad things only happen to bad people, and good things happen to good people. There's even a theory, formulated by philosopher Melvin J. Lerner, called Belief in a Just World, where individuals assume they receive what they deserve and deserve what they receive.

Lerner states that, in reality, the world is not as fair as we would like it to be. People who work hard often receive the recognition they deserve, but not always. Individuals with little merit sometimes surpass others in opportunities. So, it's not obvious to conclude that simply doing your job will validate your efforts. This has become even more apparent in a world where people are increasingly vocal. Those who speak about their work and showcase what they do are seen and valued more, even if they are not the best at it. And the best are not necessarily seen. Therefore, even if you are an excellent professional, it's important to take responsibility for making your work visible.

"I don't want to expose my private life"

"You need to humanize your Brand, and for that, you have to show your personal life." Perhaps you've heard this phrase before, as it's tirelessly repeated by certain digital marketing gurus. While it may be valid for some types of businesses, it isn't true for everyone. The argument for using personal life content may be that such content attracts huge attention, especially the coveted "likes" on social media (otherwise, shows like Big Brother wouldn't have the numerical impact they do). However, being highly visible doesn't necessarily build the attributes you desire for your Personal Brand. This attraction, driven more by human curiosity than value exchange, is favorable to professional categories that thrive on buzz and need this effect to stay in the limelight.

The fact that many people have liked, commented, and shared a post doesn't necessarily mean that you are having a positive, meaningful construction for your Personal Brand strategy.

We've lost count of the number of people who come to us and explicitly ask if it's possible to work on their brand without feeling invaded by exposure. This concern is more than legitimate, and yes, there are other ways to humanize your brand. We can already say that choosing certain aspects of your personal life to share is different from sharing your intimate life, as we will see later when we talk about communication.

"I've invested a lot in my current Brand"

When we learn something new about ourselves or reframe what we already know, we may feel the urge to show ourselves to the world from this new perspective. But sometimes, we hold back this change due to a strong attachment to what we have built thus far. Is it worth abandoning a consolidated position and investing in communicating a change? There's a concept called sunk cost, used in the financial market, which we can adapt to Personal Brand. In the financial market, this term is used when you buy a stock and its value plummets. In this case, it's not worth wasting time waiting for the value to return to the previous level. It's recommended to accept the loss and sell. In the case of Personal Brand, it's futile to try to recover what already has more value or no longer makes sense for who you are today. That's a waste of time. Honoring your entire trajectory, it's important to understand that now is the time to invest in communicating what makes you who you are today. Therefore, it will make more sense to work on your Personal Brand with a focus on the future you want to build for yourself.

Lara is a consultant, whose company was almost an extension of her corporate life. Her experience in strategic planning in large companies naturally led her to work in consulting in this area, attracting clients seeking her expertise. When she decided to make a huge career shift and study nutrition, she faced many questions: "Are you going to abandon everything you've built so far? Are you going to start over from scratch?" Besides the insecurity of knowing she would have to give up recurring revenue from projects based on her established expertise, and have to heavily invest in a new area, she was also dealing with the social pressure generated by her choice.

Lara, however, was determined, and doing financial acrobatics to complete the new course, she made the decision we consider the most appropriate: she started working on her new positioning from the first day of college. The result? Lara graduated with a waiting list for her practice. We're not saying it's easy to make this shift. What caught our attention was the self-confidence that gave her focus to build a strong message.

Therefore, detachment seems to be a very good word to translate the concept of sunk cost. Let go of everything you have invested in so far, and only make a decision or take the next step of your brand looking forward, towards the future and the goals you want.

My Personal Branding process, led by BetaFly, was an extraordinary inner journey. I sincerely never thought I could extract so much value from my persona, and I can only express my gratitude for Susana's patience, perseverance, generosity, and understanding. She navigates and delves deep into your personality through thought-provoking questions to bring out your best, enhancing self-awareness and dispelling any fears you may have about expressing your personal brand.

Highly perceptive in her technique, she always goes beyond expectations, following a well-structured process to ensure the focus on identifying the essence of your brand is never lost. It's brilliant how she lays out all the branding concepts on the table. The result is a clear brand direction, almost effortlessly. This is accompanied by great support from the team, making the entire process much more convenient.

Jaime Castromil,
COO Latin America - Deutsche Bank

CHAPTER 4

FROM CORPORATE BRAND
TO PERSONAL BRAND

The origin of the word "Brand" couldn't be clearer in what it represents. "Brand" comes from the Old Norse "brandr," which means "torch" or "fire." The term was gradually adapted into Old English as "brand," which also referred to a torch but acquired another meaning: that of a mark made with a hot iron on animals, used to identify the ownership or origin of the animal. Therefore, "brand" also refers to the branding iron – and the first known brands in history were born out of this need: to mark the origin of products to attest to their quality. When Branding became a discipline, authors referred to this mark left as something impactful, something that literally "brands." Hence, it remains in memory.

One of the greatest authors on this topic, Jean Noel Kapferer, said that "a brand is a name that influences consumers". This idea was purely commercial, considering that a consumer may value, prefer, and even pay more for a product from a well-known brand. From this came the concept that a strong brand allows for a differentiated market position and, therefore, has financial value. This is what we call "brand equity = brand value." Therefore, a brand is a valuable intangible asset.

There are several definitions of what a brand is, and none alone is complete enough to fully explain a subject with such a high degree of subjectivity. This subjectivity happens because a brand is composed of a set of factors that, together, build an emotional connection with the public it interacts with. They can be visuals like packaging, colors, and design, activating other senses with components like smell, ambiance, and decoration. Added to all this is the main element that forms a brand, which is the public's experience with it – this is what will strongly impact the value of what it delivers.

Every experience generates a **perception**. In turn, that perception generates a **future expectation**. Therefore, a brand also carries an implicit promise that future interactions with it will be similar to past experiences. Thus, what builds a strong brand is a succession of experiences people have with it over time. Think of any product, for example, wine. If a winery has a tradition of making good wines, even though each vintage presents its own characteristics, the enthusiasts of that brand become accustomed to a certain standard and expect that the winery's future wines will also be good. This expectation was formed by the characteristics of the wines already produced by the winery.

These characteristics are called **brand attributes**, which are adjectives, such as person, product, or service, we associate with a brand. In the case of wine, we say it is "full-bodied" or "elegant."

When I, Giuliana, had the opportunity to work with the Havaianas brand, I experienced this care in ensuring that the brand's experience reinforces its attributes. The Havaianas flagship store on Oscar Freire Street in São Paulo represents a brand experience that goes beyond simply selling flip-flops and other products. There, you can "feel" and "experience" all the brand's attributes. The store is a **physical representation of the brand**, an environment that engages and connects consumers to all the attributes of Havaianas. At the entrance, you are immediately struck by a large, colorful panel and feel a pleasant aroma in the air, specially developed for the store. The uniforms of the salespeople were designed to convey relaxation, lightness, and comfort. The hired salespeople aim to showcase Brazilian culture in all its forms. The spacious, well-lit atmosphere with many tropical plants and market stalls to display the flip-flops creates a cheerful and casual atmosphere, accompanied by Brazilian music played at a pleasant volume. The experience of customizing the flip-flop reinforces another brand attribute, that of being democratic: for everyone and all tastes. The ability to customize your own flip-flop reinforces another brand attribute, that of being democratic: for everyone and all tastes. It's impossible not to be impacted by the brand's attributes, even implicitly, when visiting the store.

The future expectation of a brand can also come through association. When we enter a restaurant, for example, the communication codes used by the establishment - décor, service, music, lighting, etc. - automatically set our expectations at a certain level. Notice that these expectations are formed implicitly. Just being in a certain environment begins to shape them in our minds. In this case, the restaurant may not have explicitly promised anything, but the person already imagines what to expect based on the signals given by the brand attributes. This expectation is further reinforced when the person has already had experiences with products and services that have similar proposals and similar attributes.

If we go to eat a sandwich at a food truck, we won't expect the delivery to be a gastronomic experience with the same refinement as a fancy restaurant but rather something with attributes similar to what we would expect from the category of "street food." And the experience can be very satisfying within this different expectation. Now, what will be crucial to strengthen a brand is its delivery and its performance. If an establishment communicates something and the customer has a different experience, there are three possible scenarios:

1. **the delivery meets the created expectation** – confirming that brand attribute;

2. **the delivery positively surprises, being better than expected** – enhancing the attribute;

3. **the delivery falls short of what is desired** – modifying the attribute to a lower level of expectation.

To build a positive reputation based on experience, it is important to have a strategy, regardless of the nature of the brand - whether it's a product, a service, or a person. This strategy should not just remain on paper but be consistently implemented at all touchpoints of the brand with its audiences. This succession of interactions, consistently, will form the attributes and generate the experience that will shape the reputation. Do you know which attributes immediately come to mind when people hear your name?

The Emergence of Personal Brand

The parallel between general brand concepts and personal brands results from an evolution in thinking about Marketing and Branding, an application that began throughout the 20th century. There is no specific person to whom we can accredit the created concept of Personal Brand. Although Al Ries and Jack Trout introduced the idea of positioning your personal or professional identity in the 1981 book *Positioning: The Battle for Your Mind*, the origin of the concept of Personal Brand is often attributed to Tom Peters. When he published his landmark article titled "The Brand Called

You" in *Fast Company* magazine in October 1997, Peters captured this trend and brilliantly synthesized it, revolutionizing the way we see our place in the business environment. He stated that we should assume our position as CEOs of our own company, which he calls "Me Inc.," and that the most important task of every professional is to "be the CEO" of their own brand.

Recognizing that we live in an era where individuals can take center stage alongside corporate brands, we consider this article to remain completely relevant and inspiring to everyone working with the topic.

In his book *The Brand You 50 (Reinventing Work): Fifty Ways to Transform Yourself from an "Employee" into a Brand That Shouts Distinction, Commitment, and Passion!* (1999), Peters revisits this theme by pointing out that the model of an employee working for a company was becoming outdated. He believed that it was essential for each person to position themselves as their own "brand," considering how to add value to the company using their specific set of skills and continuously updating themselves.

" THE MOST IMPORTANT TASK OF EVERY PROFESSIONAL IS TO BE THE CEO OF THEIR OWN BRAND."

Tom Peters

Daniel Goleman's classic book *Emotional Intelligence* (1995), also addressed the topic: "When you take the time to seek answers and define what makes you a unique individual, not only will you be able to build a strong Personal Brand, but you will also increase your level of self-awareness. And that is fundamental for living a fulfilling life."

Fun fact, it is very common to utilize English terms, even when speaking in other languages, to describe all that we have just explained. That's why you hear or read the expression "Personal Branding" constantly being used to refer to the process of managing your own brand.

The undeniable advantage of English is that it indicates something that endures. Since the suffix "ING" can correspond to the gerund in English, the word "Branding" in Portuguese would mean something like "Managing the Brand," indicating something that follows a continuous flow. This concept is interesting because brand management is a **construction** that unfolds over time. It is not something done once but rather a process. We also like this because the idea of this flow connects with our deep belief that being alive means being in motion and continually improving ourselves.

In summary, the concepts we described earlier about brands apply to all of your Personal Brands.

Therefore, Personal Brand is the result of how you present yourself to the world and how you are perceived by others when you take action. From the initial contact, people already form a first impression, voluntarily or involuntarily, based on the information you transmit thus forming an implicit promise. Attributes of a Personal Brand can be adjectives like "competent," "insightful," "kind," and so on. An example of this is when we're recommended a professional or service. Let's say a friend tells another: "Dr. Marcela is careful, attentive, and explains each procedure and the use of each product, including the correct order and amount. She's a very good doctor. This results in the friend receiving the recommendation to go to the doctor's office with the expectation of having the same experience, or even better. If Dr. Marcela can sustain this level of attention and care, and continually surpass expectations with each experience, she reinforces her brand attributes, which will stick in the minds of patients, clients, and her team.

That's why we always emphasize that perception is formed at all touchpoints the public has with your Personal Brand and not necessarily just when they are in your presence or interacting with you. In the example of Dr. Marcela, it is essential that she maintains a positive perception in any interaction with the patient. How they are welcomed in the office, how they perceive the sensory aspects of the environment, such as the scent, lighting, decor, colors, and even a WhatsApp message with the patient can reinforce each attribute of the brand.

Our actions are a result of everything that makes up who we are - identity, values, skills, and experiences. When we have these elements mentally organized into a defined strategy, they can become brand attributes that strengthen our Personal Brand positively. This puts us on the path to being perceived for who we are and how we wish to be seen. Therefore, it is crucial to understand, prioritize, and enhance your brand attributes to communicate them coherently and consistently.

The Challenge of Building a Memorable Personal Brand

Our recent memory capacity is limited considering the huge amount of information we accumulate, especially in a world overloaded with data, novelties, and a deluge of impacts that overwhelms us. As a result, we rarely manage to memorize the complete history of someone else's life. It's no wonder we forget much of what we hear, even when we find the content extremely interesting. Add to this the fact that, most of the time, each person is busy storing data relevant to their own existence and survival. People spend their days thinking about their own issues, desires, and ambitions. Therefore, when it comes to your Personal Brand, the chances of people keeping the details of your professional life years, explanations of where your experiences come from, and the intricacies of how you prepared to stand before them, whether in a lecture or a meeting, fresh in their mind are slim.

So, how do you keep the best attributes of your Personal Brand alive in people's minds?

Carmen Simon, a Cognitive Neuroscience specialist from California, has spent the last decade trying to perfect the answer to this question. She assists major companies in developing their communication guidelines, with strategies based on science, that can influence consumer memory about a message. One of her quotes is, "You cannot survive in the market if you're not in people's minds." Carmen is fascinated with studying memory and, despite her long-term research, is still amazed at how quickly the human brain forgets. This happens because the brain is designed to conserve energy, which it does by forgetting information deemed unnecessary or already assimilated. So, how do we increase the odds of being remembered?

I, Giuliana, had the pleasure of attending one of Carmen's classes here in California, where she explained, based on her years of neuroscience research, that our brain only records relevant information that taps into our emotions, sensations, and experiences. The more content triggers emotions, the more likely it is to be imprinted in the mind. That's precisely how a brand embeds itself in people's minds: through the perceptions created with each experience. Thus, it's the deliveries, services, products, experiences... that will make you relevant. And it's up to you to direct that content in the way you want to be remembered.

A quote attributed to Maya Angelou says, "People will forget what you said, people will forget what you did, but they will never forget how you made them feel." We can then say that others will primarily hold onto something about you that is connected with an emotion, something they deemed relevant, or both, from their experience with you. The attributes people assign to you result from their conclusions about the quality of what you presented, combined with how you made them feel: and that is what will constitute the residual memory of your Personal Brand. This summary defines you in another person's mind

> **❝❝ PEOPLE WILL FORGET WHAT YOU SAID, PEOPLE WILL FORGET WHAT YOU DID, BUT THEY WILL NEVER FORGET HOW YOU MADE THEM FEEL."**
>
> Maya Angelou

and simplifies the decisions they will make going forward in relation to what you offer.

That's why we say that brands act as shortcuts the brain uses to avoid having to reassess a person at every interaction. To compare it to a commonplace scenario: imagine you are at the supermarket and you need to buy a particular product. Consider the shelf filled with various items. How do you choose? You're not likely to want to read every label to understand the differences in detail. Typically, the first thing we do is look for known brands, and names that assure us that the product will be good.

That's what we mean by "shortcuts": familiar names that assure us we're making a safe choice. If we think this way about purchasing a mundane product, consider when we're talking about hiring someone to help us with something more complex. It's important to remember that anything that happens frequently reinforces a mental trigger called "confirmation bias," which makes people expect the pattern to continue and look for signs confirming their expectations.

Here's how it works:

1. A person behaves in a certain way consistently, thereby creating an image of themselves in the minds of others.

2. This presumption spreads, and people start looking for evidence to confirm it.

3. Even if there are few facts to support this assumption, people cling to them because it is mentally more comfortable to confirm something known rather than come up with something new. People look for mental shortcuts that confirm their beliefs. A brand is a shortcut. Any brand. Examples include thoughts like

"This man is sophisticated," "These clothes are quality," "This team is competent," and "This hotel provides good service."

4. Any sign that confirms our perception becomes "proof" that mentally reinforces our thesis.

Working on the attributes of your Personal Brand is about making life easier for others so that they can remember everything you can bring to their lives. It's almost like putting into other people's mouths the key aspects by which you'd like your name to be remembered. Hence the famous phrases "help me remember you," or, "make it easy to choose you," or even "remind me that you exist, remind me of what you can do for me." The goal is for you to build trust in what can be expected from your work. When people are faced with a choice, your name should sound familiar, comfortable, and safe.

Personal Brand is about connection and trust

While conceptually the principles used to work with corporate brands and Personal Brands are very similar, managing Personal Brands is a bit more specific. This is because we are dealing with human beings and not companies, products, or services. The relationships we establish from person to person have a deeper and subtle meaning. Therefore, when we think about Personal Brand, we can say that a brand is a name that generates connection and trust.

In almost every professional relationship, trust is formed through constant authentic interactions while your competent skills are highlighted when delivering results. When you act coherently and authentically, your brand attributes are conveyed truthfully, and this will generate more trust in your audiences. Similarly, what you commit to deliver creates a connection with people through the affinity of ideas, purposes, emotions provided by your brand experience, or problems you solve.

Doctors with a well-known reputation have a full schedule, regardless of what they may charge for their services. A prestigious executive receives offers for significant positions in notable companies. A strong Personal Brand influences people to make decisions, trust in their services, and be motivated to work on a particular team or project. Purchasing an idea, product, or project occurs because of the trust and connection conveyed by the Personal Brand. This happens to all of us, right? We rarely decide to close a deal without that link of trust.

When we worked at *Natura* we were able to experience this concept first-hand. At the heart of the business were thousands of sales consultants who, unknowingly, taught us the basic principles of Personal Brand management. If they all sold the same product, why did a customer buy from one consultant and not another? The so-called "relationship sale" has this concept at its core: by establishing a relationship of trust with their clients, a *Natura* consultant captivates their audience with their unique way of serving, the convenience of their delivery, or another attribute that makes them a standout professional.

With the FLY® Method, we will help you to identify your brand attributes that will establish these links with your audiences. On this journey, it will be possible to outline a communication strategy that will enable you to connect and maintain impactful and memorable experiences with your clients, stakeholders, patients, and/or colleagues. This strategic project for your Personal Brand is the journey that we invite you to embark on with us now.

I first met Giu and her work with doctors on Personal Branding a few years ago, and I was immediately excited about the idea of bringing this concept to the medical field here in Brazil. I saw a great opportunity to connect Giu with some of the projects I was leading, as the vision of our brands was remarkably aligned. I have always believed in the importance of positioning, and in all my projects and initiatives, I strive to convey the idea that each of us must find our place in the world.

In 2022, I had the pleasure of meeting Giu in person during an informal lunch, and from that encounter, many ideas emerged that turned into concrete actions a few months later. Together, we went on a tour across Brazil, impacting many Brazilian doctors and demonstrating the importance of partnerships between companies and physicians. The pharmaceutical industry plays a key role in the development of doctors by providing scientific knowledge about solutions for their patients' concerns.

With Giu's support, I was able to spread the idea that the industry can also help doctors build connections and view medicine as a structured business. A great way to start this transformation is by looking inward, understanding the purpose of each practice, and effectively communicating it to the market.

The partnership with Giu has brought significant results, not only for the doctors involved but also for the companies and the medical sector as a whole. We are expanding doctors' perspectives, empowering them to stand out as successful professionals, and showing that collaboration with the industry can be a beneficial strategy for all.

I am truly grateful for the opportunity to work alongside Giu on this inspiring journey, and I look forward to continuing to build positive impact together.

Caio Brabo da Silva,
Marketing Services Manager - Galderma

CHAPTER 5

FLY® METHOD FOR
PERSONAL BRANDING

Throughout our lives, we build and strengthen our Personal Brand through our actions and therefore are inseparable from it. The problem is that what we actually are isn't always perceived by others. This is why it is crucial to learn to manage your own brand. By defining your brand and controlling the narrative to strengthen it, you increase the chances of being recognized for what you wish to convey, rather than letting others establish meanings detached from who you truly are.

As Tom Peters said, "If you want people to see you as a powerful brand, act like a trustworthy leader. When you think of yourself as a brand, you don't need an organizational chart for authority to be a leader. The fact is you already are a leader. You are your own leader." Take on the responsibilities of the CEO of your brand – and remember that for this position, much like others in life, there are no shortcuts.

To assist you in organizing your Personal Brand, we developed the FLY® Method, which is the result of many years dedicated to Branding projects in our executive and advisory experience, and over 15,000 people served in various formats - mentoring, classes, lectures, and workshops.

For you to reflect on your Personal Brand and find paths from our methodology, one factor is very important: having a clear goal, something you want to achieve, a place you wish to reach. It will guide what you want to build and determine which attributes you want to add to your Personal Brand.

If you haven't thought about this yet, or if you have and want to review it, we suggest a "warm-up" by answering the following questionnaire. It will serve to deepen your reflection on your current moment. Having these written insights to refer back to will help you find solutions and insights for strengthening your Personal Brand, making it more authentic and aligned with what you wish to achieve from this work.

Practical Exercise: Warm-up

- What would you like to be remembered, recognized, chosen, and preferred for?

- What professional recognition do you believe you deserve?

- Five years from now, when someone asks you about this professional period in your life, how would you like to describe it?

- What success story do you want to tell about the life you're living now?

- What are the most relevant aspects that people need to know about you? List those elements you consider being important for your reflection in this work.

- What do you believe sets you apart from your peers as a professional?

- Is something bothering you about your Personal Brand? Or the way you believe it impacts your audiences?

This self-analysis is the starting point of your journey. To continue delving into your Personal Brand and achieving the results you desire, keep these two premises in mind:

a. Focus on the Positive

We'll shed light and direct most of our energy to what each person does best and what can be improved to make their Personal Brand shine. We prioritize this over concentrating on overcoming difficulties. Of course, people need to seek self-improvement always. However, the secret to the success of a Personal Brand is the ability to identify what you do best and apply it to daily activities. We want you to flesh out your strengths and make them even more solid.

This understanding is based on positive psychology, a discipline initiated by Martin Seligman. It teaches us the power of changing our perspective to maximize our happiness potential from our day-to-day actions. This view has been a watershed for human development disciplines because it understands the power of employing talents towards our goals and how this positive cycle has incredible potential to increase happiness and the sense of meaning in life.

b. Focus on the Future

Our focus is on what you seek and desire for your future - and on how we can help you get there. It's very easy for people to lose this reference and get drained by reflections on the past, how they got here, and what they could have done differently to achieve a better outcome. These reflections are important and valid. However, this method looks towards the future. Your past holds important learnings and experiences. Now, what will we do with all these reputational assets you've built? How can they help you achieve the goals that lie ahead? How can your work be an important pillar of a meaningful life? That's what we call focus on the future. With this mindset, it's possible to direct your energy towards building these possibilities.

By analyzing and highlighting your strengths and adding a focus on the future, we arrive at a personalized and unique analysis, which will be the foundation of your brand. As a result, there is more motivation to continue on the path and in the direction you define as the next step in your life because you'll see yourself in a very particular and powerful way, we've even seen this happen with our clients. But what will really power the method is your determination to begin and sustain work in the desired direction for your Personal Brand, with focus, clarity about your positive traits, and belief in your capacity and skills to move forward. This will make all the difference in the outcomes you can achieve.

I really enjoyed the work we did together. I had many doubts about how to manage my personal brand while being an executive at a company, but throughout the program, I refined and aligned the nuances of working on both aspects simultaneously. Rediscovering—and I could even say discovering—my strengths and unique qualities was a highlight. It's impressive how the process helped bring these elements into my positioning in a practical way.

I understood that I can enhance my positioning as an executive by leveraging my authentic values and skills with any audience. I am already seeing results when I put myself out there and engage in different environments. This is the best part—genuinely positioning myself and exposing my brand to reach new horizons, both in my executive career and toward the goals of the business I lead.

Arthur Sousa,
CEO - GDSUN

A STORY

"I knew I needed help but wasn't sure what kind. I had tried therapy, but I knew that wasn't exactly it. With the Personal Branding process, I understood how to position myself, and my career rapidly accelerated. Today, I am a CEO at a major global group, and I know that a big part of that success is because I managed to give visibility to who I am, what I believe in, and what I can do for the brands I work with."

Eugênia del Vigna - CEO Brazil - Match Group

When we began Eugênia's process, she was 38 and at a professional crossroads, eager to determine her objectives for the next cycle. She indicated how vital it was to have a clearer insight into the legacy she wanted to build from then on. Her daughter Fernanda, who was one and a half at the time, was her great motivation. "I want to be an example for my daughter," she told us.

She had been reflecting on the pivotal moments of her career, proud of some achievements and less so of others. "I think I know the kind of company I want to go to, but I need help in this process of discovering what I want for the next 20 years of my life."

HER CHALLENGES?

She wanted to overcome some past professional "frustrations," to take control in determining her direction, and to feel fulfilled. And, as a woman, overcome gender biases. Being an assertive person, she needed to be careful not to be perceived as aggressive.

"I'm halfway through my professional life, and from here on, I want to be deliberate about my decisions. It's not the position that will mean success for me. It's working for a company whose purpose I believe in. I want to feel that I've played my part. Therefore, I need a way to structure my Personal Brand and to seek the right opportunity."

THE PERSONAL BRANDING PROCESS

Right at the start of the process, the result of the 360° feedback, a self-awareness tool we use, was transformative for Eugênia to neutralize the strong lens of self-criticism. She realized how our culture generally encourages us to focus on what we need to develop rather than what we are already good at, and this had tainted her self-perception. "My self-criticism prevented me from seeing the positive aspects others saw in me."

She immediately noticed that many felt honored just for being chosen to respond to the questionnaire about her. The positive evaluation was more evident in the clear perception that Eugênia was an executive with great people management skills, extremely dedicated and committed, with an above-average capacity for organization that made her exceptionally efficient. She understood that her emotional intensity, which led her to dive wholeheartedly into what she did, was one of her greatest talents. And, like any talent, it needs to be calibrated so it doesn't become a poison. Understanding how to use her emotional intelligence to her advantage, she saw an opportunity to overcome her fears about visibility on social media.

During the process, she structured her communication to show the world not just her strategic vision, achievements, and positive leadership, but also her viewpoints. "I decided to start sharing my opinion in some posts, taking a stand. It became very clear to me the power of a well-defined stance." Having clarified the main topics for which she wanted to be recognized, her next step was to organize her networking more strategically.

With little affinity for political maneuvering, Eugenia realized that to achieve a senior position, she needed to work more on some aspects of her executive presence, specifically body language, and she invested in learning about this area. Finally, she decided to follow a wisdom that applies to almost everyone: "Stick to a path and give it time. I know my results will come."

EUGÊNIA'S RESULTS

A few months after completing her Personal Branding process, Eugênia received an offer to take on a directorial role at another company, which was much more in line with what she was looking for in life. The recruiters mentioned they were deeply impressed by some articles she had written and the clear way she expressed her viewpoints. A year later, another invitation arrived, and she became the CEO of a global group.

We're not saying that everyone who goes through a Personal Branding process will become CEOs, but stories like Eugênia's are examples of just how much organizing your narrative can clarify to those around you who you are, the value you bring to your audiences, and your unique ways of doing so. Clarity of positioning can be a lot more powerful than people tend to think.

CHAPTER 6

BEING
A BRAND

Companies, products, services—they all have brands. People, on the other hand, are their brand. The focus of our work is to bring out the Personal Brand that truly expresses who you are. So, it's not about HAVING a brand. It's about BEING a brand.

An authentic Personal Brand is expressed in a way that aligns with YOUR identity. If you do not reveal your essence, there can be no authenticity. It runs the risk of creating a character and working on a Personal Brand that will not be sustainable over time.

Therefore, the construction of a Personal Brand happens from the inside out. This method is based precisely on clarity of identity and the pursuit of expanding self-awareness. With this work, your role in the world will also become clearer to you.

Before we begin the practical process, we want to share a bit of the theory behind this dive into your identity as one of the first steps of the FLY® Method. This way, you'll understand the why's behind the method and its foundation. We start with identity studies which, as you will see in the following chapters, have transformed into a process with reflections that can be put into practice and bring about amazing results.

What is Identity?

Reflecting on oneself separate from others is relatively new in history. Although philosophical inquiries into identity date back to antiquity, according to some scholars like Durkheim, Kauffmann, and Giddens, this is a concept predominantly linked to modernity—a time when reflections about the "self" intensified. This is because in traditional cultures the individual saw themselves as part of the collective and identity changes occurred through rites of passage.

It was George Mead who formulated one of the earliest theories of what would be called Symbolic Interactionism School, proposing how the social context influenced, from childhood, a balance between the "me" and the "I". According to Mead, the child seeks feedback from trusted people, and upon hearing what they say about the child, he or she starts to adopt these attributes. What happens in the child's mind is something akin to "if they say this about 'me', then 'I' must be this way." It is in this process that the notion of "I" emerges in the human being. While "I" is the imaginative representation we have of ourselves, the "me" is the adaptive attitude we have towards the world. As the "I" matures, it learns to counterbalance the influence of the "me", or how other people see it. The sociologist Mariana Scussel Zanatta explains how this theory connects with branding in terms of others' influence on us:

> To the process of interaction, we can link the process of recognition. Recognition of others and self-recognition through others. Mead (edited by Charles W. Morris, 1993) talks about 'significant others,' the people who are most often part of our interactions, with whom we maintain more intense emotional relationships. And he also identifies the 'generalized other,' defined as the organized social group, or society acting upon the individual. It is in this form, as the generalized other, that social processes influence individual behavior."

The sense of Identity is dynamic, and it develops through this continuous conversation between the "I" and the "me", defining how it preserves or changes itself. Giddens placed the theme of reflexivity at the central axis of his theory on Identity: we are continuously interacting with others and ourselves. Through this conversation, we define our identity slice, who and how we are in the world. A being is not static; it keeps internal and external dialogues and is constantly changing.

Put simply, we are constantly comparing our internal feelings of who we are with the perception others communicate to us. And what enables this interaction with others is language, both verbal and nonverbal communication. For many authors, social interaction and communication are synonymous:

> *The importance of language to social interaction is indicated by the fact that communication and social interaction are virtually synonymous for many, and by the fact that language is typically seen as the primary vehicle of human communication. As social, language is a system of significant symbols.*

In 1967, Frank Dance wrote that communication is not static; it is always moving in the direction of time. Communication demands time, as described by Sá Martino:

> *Imagine yourself in a conversation. The remarks of each speaker, at the same time, alter and are altered by the others. Not only is the question changed by the answer, but with each phrase, the speakers are different from what they were the moment before. Each statement in a conversation introduces a host of previously unknown information, whether deliberately or not.*

Identity, therefore, is a continuous internal conversation in which you draw conclusions about yourself, based on what you feel and the exchanges you have with people. Since we are beings in constant evolution, this process continues throughout our lives. And so we continue, maturing in some aspects, strengthening certain pronounced personality traits, softening others, but we never cease to be who we are. We maintain an essence that provides coherence through all the changes we undergo.

The Oxford English Dictionary defines 'identity' as: "The sameness of a person or thing at all times or in all circumstances; the condition or fact that a person or thing is itself and not something else." It is in this way we exist in the world that forms our Personal Brand.

That is why a Personal Brand that is guided by Identity is so strong. No matter how much time passes and how you evolve in this process, it remains authentic.

Expansion of Self-Awareness

Many other authors have explored Identity within the fields of Sociology and Social Psychology. For our method, we will go directly to Claude Dubar, who introduced the idea that Identity is the result of the articulation between two concepts, (i) the biographical process (what kind of person you want to be / you say you are = identity for oneself) and (ii) the relational (what kind of person you are/is said to be = identity for others). According to Dubar, identity is never fixed. It is always being constructed and must continually be reconstructed.

> This makes us aware that social identity is not as solid as we imagined, that it's not the same for our entire lives, that it can be negotiated and revoked, and that the decisions one makes, the paths one takes, the way one acts and the social worlds one belongs to are crucial factors in the identity-building process.

In our experience with the FLY® Method, we've observed the power of these reflective processes. We believe that the process of expanding consciousness about who we are and who we wish to be can be influenced by telling and retelling our own story, therefore continuously generating new perspectives.

You don't have to be an expert in these theories to ask yourself some powerful questions at some point in your life:

- In what ways do people's perceptions of me resonate with how I feel?

- What are the most active characteristics that lead people to perceive me in a particular way?

- What aspects of myself had I not realized before?

- Which facets of my Identity would I like to reveal at this stage of my life?

We call these questions "powerful" because they may seem simple at first glance, but answering them honestly requires an internal dialogue that can lead to desires for change or the reaffirmation of decisions about ourselves. As writer Naguib Mahfouz (1988) said, "You can tell how intelligent a person is by their answers. You can tell how wise a person is by their questions."

The FLY® Method for Personal Branding is just that: questions we pose to assist people in reflecting on their identity.

- Who are you?

- How do you perceive your role in the world?

- How would you like others to perceive your impact?

We ask these questions without any expectation of exhausting them. On the contrary, we hope they continue to resonate and that your answers are continually revisited. This is the beauty of Personal Branding, and what sets it apart from all other kinds of branding: we are always in motion.

To sum up our discussion on the expansion of consciousness, we'd like to leave you with a final thought:

How many times have you had to tell and retell your story throughout your life?

Certainly, countless times, and there will likely be many more instances when it will be necessary to do so. Perhaps you're in a new environment, pursuing new goals, changed companies, or, like me, Giuliana, starting a new life in a different country. The truth is that our story is constantly evolving, and it's important to be willing to adapt and share it as changes occur in our lives.

How Your Personal Brand is Formed from Identity

Our Identity lives within us. No one can guess just by looking if a person is competent, ethical, or reliable. A well-known quote from the book The Little Prince says: "What is essential is invisible to the eye."

The way to make the invisible visible is by taking action in the world. Imagine an image of an iceberg. What is below the water is your Identity, made up of your essence, beliefs, values. What is above the surface is what is seen, the conscious level. It is the way you show the world your Identity by using your brand attributes, behavior, communication, and experience. Today, you may be talking to someone. Tomorrow, speaking on a program or podcast. The day after, writing an article, giving a lecture, participating in a meeting, and in each of these interactions, letting the other person know a little more about your Identity. As we act, we express ourselves, and even when we are silent, we send signals about our essence. In this way, people observe, feel, and draw conclusions about our Identity.

Various studies say that when we meet someone for the first time, our brain quickly forms an impression of that person in a fraction of seconds. Many will say that this first impression is almost definitive. In some situations, it may be true. In some circumstances, such as a job interview or a meeting at an event, there is not much time to convey everything that needs to be conveyed. That is why there are numerous courses and tips on how to dress, how to speak, and how to make a positive first impression. These physical aspects are indeed relevant, but when we think about strengthening your Personal Brand in the medium and long term, they are not absolute or definitive. Other variables will contribute to the formation of this brand.

If you have the opportunity to interact a little more with a person, such as in a presentation, a chat, or even in a recorded video, all the attributes that you can communicate through your content and how you present your content will form an image of you in the other person's mind. It is quite common for us to use expressions like "I had a good impression of Joana." An impression has this sense of being something static, a snapshot or photo. However, a first impression can be confirmed or deconstructed as "I interact more with Joana."

If Joana is someone who consistently behaves with competency, the attribute "competent" will stick in people's minds when they think of Joana. After all, she was not competent just once or twice – she is generally competent. Therefore, Personal Branding is not formed by a single impactful moment which some people are constantly preparing. It is formed over time. It is by grouping meanings that people mentally associate attributes with your name. If an impression is like a photo, the reputation formed by the sum of these photos is a movie.

This chart shows how this process happens in an ascending manner, starting from within (Identity), passing through the image (impact on others), and forming reputation (what they think about us).

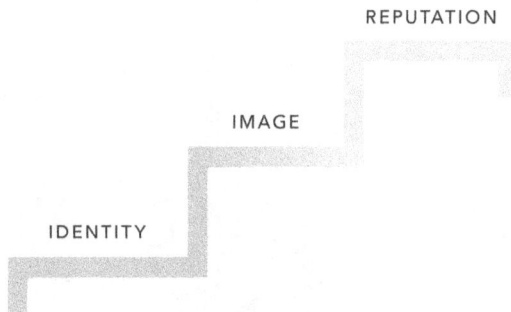

REPUTATION

IMAGE

IDENTITY

Understanding that your Identity is the foundation of the FLY® Method for Personal Branding journey is the first step. Some may seek us out wanting to skip this step and go directly to solving their communication problem, which includes writing articles, posting on social media, and networking. Often these people are filled with insecurities and doubts because they don't know how or what to communicate. The key to making communication flow is to first look at Identity, which involves diving deeper. Then, define Brand DNA and Positioning. The final step is Communication Strategy, which will be a consequence of everything discovered, reflected upon, and worked on. By following these steps, it will be much easier to define what, how, where, and why to communicate. Our guidance is always to go through the complete journey to have more consistency, authority, and authenticity in communicating your brand.

Susana Arbex's workshop started off provocatively with her explanation of the concept:

"Personal Brand is what people say about you when you're not in the room."

With this direct and impactful language, I was prompted to reflect on the messages I am conveying and how I want to be perceived. I continue to reflect because Susana sparked a process within me—a process that goes beyond the messages I project. It also involves recognizing the potential I already have but haven't yet shown, allowing me to acknowledge and embrace my talents.

"Impactful and profound" perfectly describe this moment, yet it was also light and enjoyable.

Today, I've already taken on another challenge, but I keep reflecting because I understand that this is a continuous process—what messages am I projecting, what messages do I want to convey, and what potential within me can I allow myself to fully live out.

It was so transformative that I still remember Susana's words to this day.

I am deeply grateful!

Elisabete Mercadante,
Educacional Designer

A STORY

"The process I went through with Betafly went far beyond just working on Personal Branding and setting up a communication flow and thought leadership. I was provoked to reflect on my professional journey, refine my ambitions, and paths for future development. And, at the end of it, turn all these learnings and reflections into a clear strategic positioning. The process inspired me to express myself more, write better, and break the barriers and prejudices that we executives still have about having a more personal, active voice and genuinely acting as ambassadors of our personal legacy and the companies we represent."

Alexandre Correa - CEO Gerdau Graphene

When we met Alexandre in 2019, we immediately felt that we were in the presence of a person overflowing with energy. His speech shows passion for the new, for the future, for what is not yet, but can be. He is one of those people with such a quick mind that speech can barely keep up.

In his professional journey, he has experienced diverse roles such as Risk, Logistics, and Marketing at Unilever, Operations at Lacoste,

Trade at Havi, and creating an innovative fluff cellulose business from scratch at Suzano - among others. He closed commercial deals in over 20 countries worldwide and has no fear of exploring and opening new markets wherever they may be.

Between 2015 and 2020, he made an interesting career shift from the B2C universe to diving into the B2B world - which he fell in love with. His work transitioned from a mass-market brand communication and statistical commercial approach to a demand for a more direct and personal brand communication and positioning.

As this professional shift was happening, he was also aware of another movement: the maturation of digital networks, which led executives in Brazil to begin understanding the value of positioning themselves as ambassadors of their companies, brands, and legacies. He had a huge curiosity to understand more about the value and process of building a Personal Brand and that's how he found us. Meanwhile, in his personal life, the passion for cooking for friends, traveling, exploring new cultures, and the enchantment with his newborn daughter intertwined.

HIS CHALLENGES?

Organizing the narrative of this multi-faceted career around the axis that unites them: innovation. Alexandre has always imprinted something innovative in all his experiences. The strong influence of his mother, a great researcher, made him a person with an open mind and an exploratory spirit. But he felt that the market was too accustomed to putting people in "boxes" by industry: logistics, finance, etc. His desire was to leave a Personal Brand and a legacy, being an executive who presents unknown solutions or what he believes to be impossible, transforming the markets where he operates.

THE PERSONAL BRANDING PROCESS

Early on in the reflections on the Brand DNA, we identified the key talents as: Achievement, Activation, Focus, and Future Vision. In other words, these were the characteristics that marked your work performance in all areas and companies.

The respondents of the 360° Feedback associated the characteristics of "Entrepreneur" with Alexandre, considering him a person with the skills of "Visualizing the future" and "Making the vision happen."

How can all of this be presented in a way that makes sense? The answer, brought by him throughout the reflections, couldn't have been more assertive: I am an intrapreneurial and ambidextrous executive.

Intrapreneurial, because Alexandre is able to implement innovation practices within the structures of organizations he passes through. He is not the solo entrepreneur of a startup, but an internal transformation agent in organizations.

Ambidextrous is defined as one who writes with both the right and left hand. An ambidextrous executive is one who can transition not only between distinct areas like Marketing and Logistics but also between the conceptual and the practical, the vision of the future and the problem that needs to be solved today, the collective and the individual. A subtle, delicate balance that is very difficult to find, especially in a polarized world like the one we live in.

RESULTS FOR ALEXANDRE

We arrived at a powerful, precise, and potent Brand Positioning: "I help companies identify opportunities and turn them into new businesses and products. Additionally, I structure their entire value chain and market route by implementing the most modern B2C practices in the B2B universe with a global perspective, having already developed businesses serving markets as distinct as Japan, China, France, and the USA simultaneously. And I empower multifunctional teams to deliver this disruption sustainably."

Today, Alexandre is the CEO of Gerdau Graphene, a globally active company that leads cutting-edge research in nanomaterials, offering the market a new material, graphene, which is revolutionizing the industry as we know it by reconciling something that seemed impossible: increased performance with less environmental impact. Alexandre's story shows how one's essence can unfold in different positions and challenges in a professional life. After all, being consistent does not mean being predictable.

CHAPTER 7

BRAND
DNA

DNA contains the genetic information of each individual, storing and transmiting instructions. Technically speaking, its structure is so effective and well-refined for this transmission that over evolutionary time, it has become the universal data storage molecule for all forms of life. It is responsible for sending instructions so that our body functions in a specific way.

In a very simplistic analogy, we can say that our Identity is like our DNA. Our Identity spends its entire life sending information so that we behave the way we are. The fact that DNA— and Identity— are constants does not mean they are static. They are a "conductor," allowing flexibility, which is natural and expected in the development of a human being. I, Susana, have always been Susana. However, the Susana at 50 is different from the Susana at 35, who is different from the Susana at 20. It would be strange if it wasn't that way, and if, at 50, I were thinking and behaving exactly as I did at 20. Maturity reinforces some attitudes, discards others, and incorporates new ones. These changes are part of a natural dynamic.

The process in the FLY® Method unfolds around the Brand DNA. In the illustration below, we show the step-by-step construction of this initial stage. Do not worry if you have any doubts. Our intention now is only to show the mental map, a summary of the journey we will take.

So, let's see: in a quick presentation, our path begins by making a fundamental triangulation for our work:

- What do you offer to the world? (Your Talents)

- How do you perceive your performance? (Your Self-Perception)

- How do other people perceive your performance? (360° Feedback)

116

By comparing the answers to these three questions, we will have the diagnosis of your Brand.

Next, we will compare the diagnosis with how you would like people to perceive your performance, using the Johari Window tool.

We will reflect on:

- Your values

- What puts you in Flow

Putting all of this together, you can elaborate on:
- Your vision

- Your Purpose

And we will close all the cornerstones of your brand using the Golden Circle structure.

We will detail each of these steps of your brand's DNA in the following chapters.

Brand DNA

BRAND DIAGNOSIS

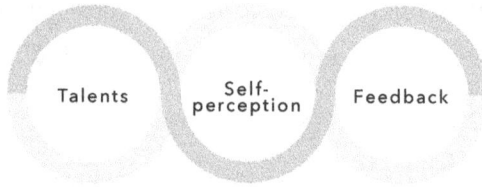

Talents	Self-perception	Feedback

↓

Closing Your Brand Diagnosis

JOHARI WINDOW

↓

INSIGHTS

↓

MAPPING THE DNA

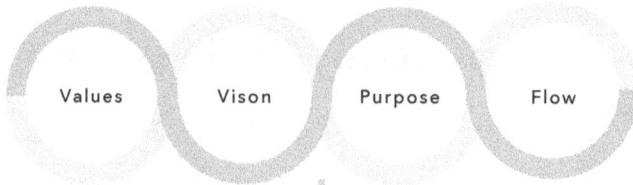

Values	Vison	Purpose	Flow

↓

GOLDEN CIRCLE

=

FOUNDATIONS OF THE PERSONAL BRAND

Brand Diagnosis

As writer José Saramago says, "We need to leave the island to see the island. We do not see ourselves if we do not go out of ourselves." So, we will start mapping the current state of your Personal Brand with this exercise: being your own object of study.

To have a successful Personal Brand in all dimensions that the word "success" includes, both personal fulfillment and professional recognition, you first need to know yourself. Then, you need to admire yourself and be able to have a powerful narrative about the value you generate.

Most of the time, we only see a part of what the world sees about ourselves. It's like looking in a mirror: we can't have a 360° view. What we see is real, but it's not one hundred percent of the truth. To fully understand our Personal Brand, we also need to visualize what is perceived about us. If you only rely on self-assessment, you will have a view of only half of your Personal Brand image. To see the other half, you need to understand what those around you think about you.

It's not very common for us to seek and/or receive truly honest feedback about the attributes of our Personal Brand, and that is what we will work on in this phase. We will capture what you have accumulated as reputational capital so far, that being what people think about you. This capital is especially marked by the most recent experiences, which are more easily accessible in the minds of people, and by the most intense experiences, which have left strong memories regardless of time.

It is important to emphasize that your Personal Brand is already out in the world, already being perceived by people. From this, you have some results that may or may not meet your expectations. So, it's time to look at the present. Your brand is alive and dynamic, so at each stage of your life, there may be some nuances more pronounced than others. How is it right now? What do you perceive? And what do others perceive? It is important to answer these questions in a structured way and in service of the branding process. Get it out of your mind and organize it. To do this Diagnosis, which is a snapshot of the present moment, you can rely on three aspects:

1. **Knowledge of your talents.** Our talents are the foundation for building our Personal Brand. It is based on what we do exceptionally well that we have a better chance to shine.

2. **Self-perception.** Even if you have never gone through any formal self-awareness process, life and the people around you give you direct and indirect feedback. Along with your ability to examine yourself, you can have a vision of yourself.

3. **Perception of others.** The Personal Brand, although originating within us, is kept alive in the hearts and minds of those who know us. You need to know what they think in order to build an effective brand plan that allows you to achieve your goals.

By combining these three dimensions, we can put together a picture of what is happening with your Personal Brand today. In other words, how you put your talents into play and how this is perceived by the audiences with whom you interact. We will then understand how much your self-analysis aligns with what others think of you.

Knowing Your Talents

When we talk about talents, we refer to those abilities that each person has since birth and executes exceptionally well. Psychologist and researcher Donald O. Clifton, Ph.D., explains in his book *Discover Your Strengths*: "Talent is any recurring pattern of thought, feeling, or behavior that can be productively applied." Therefore, it comes from those behavioral traits that come to us more easily and usually manifest since an early age. And we are all born with a propensity to do something more easily.

Talents are different from learned or acquired skills, and it is on talent we should build our Personal Brand. With talent, we have a better chance to shine much more than trying to develop what is not natural to us. Knowing your talents, therefore, is related to the premise of focusing on the positive that our method supports.

When we use our energy in favor of what we do well, the tendency is to have extraordinary results. On the other hand, when we use our energy trying to improve what we are not naturally good at, we end up making a disproportionate effort to advance, or even just managing damage control. We do improve, of course, but we rarely reach excellence – and that can lead to significant frustration. So, strive to be your best version by leveraging what you are already good at instead of trying to be a worsened version of someone else. Your uniqueness is your greatest value.

A curious fact is that, as we are usually very accustomed to what we do with ease, we often do not recognize it as a skill, a differentiator. This generates two effects:

- **First effect:** we underestimate ourselves, thinking we have no differentiator. We act using a certain talent so naturally and spontaneously that we don't even realize it is a talent.

- **Second effect:** expecting people to have the same ease as us or even belittling what we do well precisely because it does not seem difficult to us. One tip we always give to our clients is: if you get frustrated and irritated when someone has a hard time doing something you find very easy, observe yourself. Perhaps this "something" that seems so simple to you is a talent that you are not yet noticing.

The difficulty in recognizing what we are good at stems from our upbringing. Many of us were raised with the logic of overcoming our weaknesses. From school, and even in our professional activities, we were often encouraged to set aside what we do very well and focus our energy on what we need to develop.

Márcio is a CEO who has had a brilliant career. His exceptional analytical ability and strong execution discipline make him a successful professional. When we received the results of his feedback, all his skills and talents were detailed there. Everyone recognized how unique he was. But one point caught our attention: there were frequent mentions of a certain impatience. We know that the pragmatism of people in high leadership positions often leads to this trait appearing quite frequently. People want to optimize their time, so when a team member starts talking about something, this leader already imagines how it will end and wants to "save time" by interrupting the conversation. With Márcio, it was no different, and the description was confirmed by him. We could even say with a certain sense of pride. When we talked about talents and asked if he recognized in himself a tendency to look for "clones" to fill roles on his team, Márcio's pupils dilated. Being an extremely intelligent individual, he quickly understood our point: for his Personal Brand to shine and for him to have more time to focus on what he does best, it was very important to seek a team with a diversity of talents, meaning people who excel at what he does not. This way, he could dedicate himself with more focus on generating value in what truly sets him apart.

Therefore, strengthening your Personal Brand involves an intelligent balance between (I) how much energy we will put into developing what we are not good at, and (II) how much energy we will put into enhancing what we already excel at to become references. It is no coincidence that renowned NYU Stern marketing professor Scott Galloway stated in his famous advice for young people looking to succeed in their careers:

> *"Don't follow your passion." In his words, "your career should be something that brings you some pleasure, but do not confuse focus with your 'passion'. People who tell you to follow your passion are already rich: follow your talent. Being great at something (relevance, admiration, camaraderie, money) will make you fall in love with whatever it is. The path to success starts with a focus on your talent."*

If you are having trouble identifying your talents, we recommend the Gallup Clifton Strengths assessment, which highlights your top 5 talents and provides guidance on how to turn them into strengths in your Personal Brand.

Self-Perception

We all have a perception of ourselves. Whether out of curiosity or necessity, some people invest deeply in journeys of self-discovery through courses, therapies, assessment tools, and more. Additionally, those who work in companies and other organizations may have the chance to undergo processes of self-perception improvement. Even those who have never done anything of this sort usually have an opinion about themselves, which forms intuitively. For Personal Branding work, it's important to structure this perspective. Therefore, in this stage, you will engage in an exercise, creating a map of what you see in yourself. The focus will be on looking at yourself seeking the brand attributes that you consider relevant to strengthen your Personal Brand in your field of work.

Practical Exercise: Developing a Base Questionnaire

We suggest creating what we call a Base Questionnaire, where you list the questions you want answers to. It's important to first think about the answers you seek and then formulate questions that lead to them. These questions may vary depending on your field of work and, most importantly, your objective.

It's important that you seek specialization in your field and your current situation, so start by answering these questions:

- What are the main attributes for professionals in my field of work?

- Which of these attributes do I consider relevant, and which ones would I like to know people's perception of me about?

- What would I like people to tell me if they knew I wouldn't react at all?

Next, create a list of points you would like to explore about your brand and formulate questions.

We've provided some examples here, but it's crucial to customize the reflection for each situation. Examples for formulating questions include:

- Words that come to mind when people think about you
- Situations in which you excel
- Communication skills
- Leadership skills
- Soft skills
- Career opportunities
- Development opportunities
- Specific aspects of your differentiation as a professional.

You can make your base questionnaire even more elaborate by mixing question formats to obtain a more powerful analysis. Our tip is to alternate between:

- **Closed questions:** with predefined answer options;
- **Open-ended questions:** without predefined answer options that allow respondents to bring insights and suggestions;
- **Projection questions:** asking respondents to make comparisons or metaphors;
- **Evaluation questions:** asking for classification or rating.

Now, answer the Base Questionnaire: how do you perceive yourself in each of these aspects? Answer everything with the utmost honesty possible. Don't lie to yourself, don't answer what you wish, but rather what you truly believe. These answers are the result of your self-perception. Keep them to compare with what will come in your 360° Feedback.

Others Perception - 360° Feedback

What impact do you, as yourself, leave? What do people say about you when you're not in the room? In other words, what **Reputation** have you already built with your journey up to now?

As you reflect on your self-perception, you begin to mentally structure your Personal Brand. Now is the time to understand how much this structure you've modeled adheres to other people's perception. And we can only know what that is in one way: asking.

We learn more about ourselves when we see ourselves through the eyes of others. We only have a good perception of who we are and how we impact the environment around us when we compare our own view of ourselves with the opinions of those who interact with us.

Remembering that a brand is about perception, it may be that people see you in a way that you consider, for example, distorted or exaggerated. What is different in this survey compared to other feedback you may have received previously is that here we are not trying to evaluate your personality or behavior. Instead, how that personality and behavior are perceived by others. We want to understand the residual effect, what remains most striking about your performance. And perception is not up for debate because it's not about who you actually are but about the interpretation the other person has, which is how they observe and filter the information you convey through words and actions.

In search of data

One of the great lessons we've learned from interacting with professionals and academics in Silicon Valley is the almost obsessive, in a good sense, search for data that underpins hypotheses. Not that we don't value intuition. We do, very much. But when it comes to looking at ourselves, it's quite natural to see with some biases. So, what we seek in feedback are confirmations that attest what we think about ourselves, or surprise us with something we didn't know. The intention of this research is literally to pull you into reality, in order to find clearer paths to enhance your strengths.

What we look for in 360° Feedback are patterns. Therefore, frequency is very important. How often do people mention certain aspects? The higher the frequency a certain attribute appears, the more times you must convey information perceived by people in that way. Therefore, it's important to have a minimum number of people responding so that we can eliminate extremes. We consider extremes anything that, in some aspect, "pulls" your feedback to one side of the scale.

For example, Felipe has always received feedback about being a very confident person. In his 360° Feedback, it was no different: his self-confidence in project leadership and his calmness in handling difficult situations stood out as one of his main strengths, as mentioned by several people. However, in the field of opportunities for his development, one person mentioned that Felipe becomes destabilized and insecure when topics related to minority rights are debated. According to this person, the insecurity causes Felipe to "miss the mark" in his approach. So, is Felipe a confident person or not? Of course, yes, in the overwhelming majority of situations. The fact that a specific situation is mentioned is usually an exception that confirms the rule. These signals are important and should be considered. In market research, it's always said that a group, although small, is always representative of a number of people who must think in that way. However, what we seek here is what the majority of people see in you. We want to understand the main message your brand conveys.

For the same reason, it's important to note at which frequency an attribute appears, whether it's constant, minimal or not at all.

Let's see what happened with Fábio, a consultant in the strategic planning area. He is one of those incredible multi talented people. His ability to relate is just as relevant as his ability to think systematically. Moreover, he has the maturity to manage conflicts. When he completed the self-perception questionnaire, he pointed out that his most relevant brand characteristic, perceived by his audiences, should certainly be his ability to think strategically. Indeed, this was an attribute that appeared in his feedback. But it emerged with a low frequency. In contrast, the ability to innovate exploded in spontaneous mentions, followed by his skill with people. Fábio was surprised:

"So, people don't perceive how capable I am of contributing to discussions through my strategic thinking ability?" he asked us.

"No, that's not exactly what people are saying. They do recognize your ability to think strategically. Note that this appears in your feedback. However, two other brand attributes you possess are so much stronger that it's almost as if they 'shout' compared to the others," we explained.

This is an example of what we mean by seeking data by moving away from "guesswork." We don't expect you to be strongly surprised by the feedback. As we mentioned earlier, almost all of us have a good perception of who and how we are. Usually, what can surprise us are precisely these differences in intensity or some subtleties that may be revealing themselves in a certain phase of our lives and didn't appear in another.

We know this can be intriguing, perhaps even a little scary, but don't be intimidated by these feelings. If you feel a pit in your stomach at this stage, know that it's absolutely normal. Look at the positive side: asking for feedback frequently builds confidence and credibility because it shows that you are open to constructive criticism, seeking to improve and develop. This helps build stronger relationships with colleagues, partners, teams, and clients. Moreover, trust that the fear of the responses that come will be overcome by the gratification you'll have when reading what others have to say to you. Feedback is always a gift. The people who respond want, in some way, to help us. Some clients receive messages so profound that they become emotional. We ourselves have been moved a few times by these responses.

Approach this stage with an open mind and heart to receive what people have to say. "This feedback was the most comprehensive I've ever done in my professional life. I've participated in assessments by major consulting firms, but none were so comprehensive or gave me such a personalized view, with truly actionable insights," wrote Fábio in his report at the end of our meeting.

Practical Exercise: How to Ask for Feedback

- **Send a personal message.** If feedback is a gift, then it starts with a request. Your chance of getting responses increases if you send a personal message. Write something in your own language, in the way people are accustomed to receiving your communication. Don't be more or less formal than you usually are.

- **Choose people who have interacted with you professionally.** Send the questionnaire to those who know you and have worked with you to some extent. It's important to get responses based on real experiences rather than opinions.

- **Ensure the anonymity of the survey.** This is important so that people feel comfortable responding. So, we suggest providing a survey link that can be sent via message or email, emphasizing anonymity. Ideally, enlist the help of a third party to receive and organize the responses, ensuring this point. And make it clear to respondents that their messages will be treated with discretion, so they'll feel more comfortable giving honest testimonials.

If you can't rely on a third party, be transparent and ask for honesty anyway. Know that people may be a bit more hesitant to give some harsh feedback, but often, subtly, end up saying everything important you need to know. Just read carefully.

Set a deadline for receiving the response. It's very important to set a maximum date, and it shouldn't be too far away. From our experience, 60% of people respond within the first three days.

What if I can't ask for 360° Feedback?

If, for some reason, you can't send a feedback request to a group of people, for any reason whatsoever, we suggest doing a reduced version of this process. First, find three people you have a personal connection with and ask them for honest feedback. Base yourself on the themes we listed above and on the questions from your self-perception. Tips for this conversation to work well:

- **Ask for honesty.** Explain that the more honest it is, the more it helps you.

- **Listen.** Listen with your head, but also with your heart.

- **If it's an in-person conversation, try not to respond or justify.** You may consider it important to agree so that the person feels more at ease. Don't do that. Also, don't try to explain or justify the responses you receive.

- **Take notes.** We forget much of what we hear, so no matter how good your memory is, record it.

Closing Your Brand Diagnosis

This is one of the most important moments of the method because it's when we can analyze all the collected data and bring it to your reality and future objectives.

To close your Brand Diagnosis, it's time to cross-reference your answers with those of your respondents. Since the questions you sent to people are the same as those you answered about yourself in the self-perception exercise, you can also compare perceptions and assess how similar or different they are.

Additionally:

1. Utilize feedback from the past. If you've received feedback at other times in your life, use it to incorporate them, retrospectively considering all the moments in life when you received good feedback.

2. Seek other feedback and qualitative assessments you have.

3. Reflect on what you already know people think of you, even if you don't have formal feedback.

Then, compare the old feedback with the 360º Feedback you just received. This is another tool for mapping out your brand and defining what gives you more visibility in your professional performance.

Evaluate your talents and reflect on how you're putting them into action and the effect it has on your surroundings. In other words, analyze what people perceive you naturally do well and how this reflects on your Personal Brand.

Compare the image you project of yourself with the image perceived by your audiences, and see where the greatest convergences and divergences are.

Learning from a 360° Feedback

This is where the FLY® Method starts to take shape.

More than just data, feedback needs to generate value by providing powerful insights into how people perceive you. Moreover, when well-structured, it can help identify market opportunities, allowing you to make some adjustments to your brand to offer something unique and valuable to your audience.

When a person participates in a feedback process for the first time, they may be surprised when analyzing their results. They may make important connections about themselves, learn lessons, or even deny and reject the results.

On the other hand, those who know themselves a little better, either because they have invested in self-awareness tools or because they have participated in structured processes in the places where they have worked, may have a reaction like "I already knew all this about myself."

For both profiles, we extend an invitation: allow yourself to be surprised. Even with what you already know about yourself.

We told you about Fábio, who expected one attribute to appear more prominently than it actually did. With Juliana, it was the opposite. She was certain that her experience as an executive in oil and gas companies would appear in the feedback, but she didn't imagine that she would be considered a reference. When she received an avalanche of comments reinforcing this attribute, her reaction was one of pleasant astonishment. People's recognition was greater than she expected. And what she already knew about herself appeared with much greater intensity than she had imagined.

Another way to learn more about yourself through a 360° Feedback is through the absence of attributes. That is, through "non-response." Reflect on what you expected to receive as recognition but didn't appear. To make this reflection in a structured way, we suggest using a tool called the Johari Window, which is an exceptional tool for analyzing both personal and professional relationships.

The Johari Window is named after Joseph Luft and Harrington Ingham, using the initial syllables "Jo + Hari" from the names of the American researchers and psychologists. Its aim is to help better understand communication between interpersonal relationships. By reflecting in a structured way on the responses received and with the support of a good tool, you will increase your ability to turn insights into actions that you can implement immediately.

How to use the Johari Window

Using the data you have obtained so far, answer the questions related to each of the quadrants, always keeping in mind that the focus is to shed light on your positive aspects. We'll work on the gaps—your weaknesses—only if they are obstacles to achieving your goals.

Although the Johari Window has four quadrants, we'll use only the first three for our analysis. We don't work with the fourth quadrant because it concerns the unconscious, which is irrelevant to this analysis.

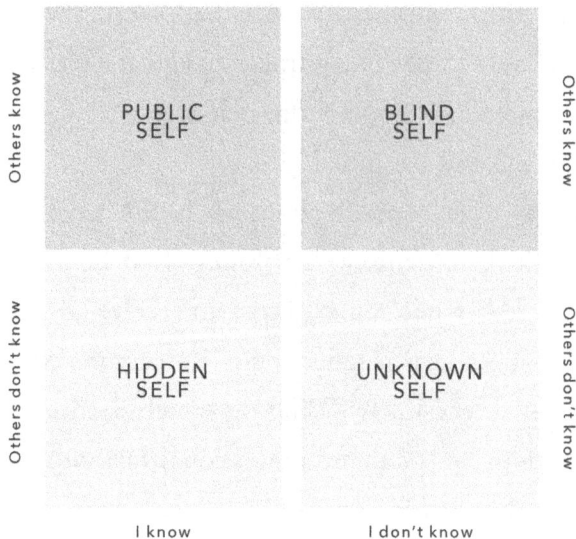

	I know	I don't know	
Others know	PUBLIC SELF	BLIND SELF	Others know
Others don't know	HIDDEN SELF	UNKNOWN SELF	Others don't know

"Public Self" Reflections:

- What are my most outstanding characteristics, by which people recognize me, and which I also recognize in myself?

- Which of them are relevant and appealing to the audiences I want to relate to?

- Which ones can help me differentiate positively from my colleagues/peers? In other words, which ones would I like to strengthen/explore in the next stage of my life?

"Blind Self" Reflections:

- What are my characteristics observed by people that I hadn't realized?

- What opportunities do they bring me?

- What precautions should I take?

"Hidden Self" Reflections:

- What characteristics do I recognize in myself that others don't perceive?

- Is there something I want to make more visible at this stage of my life?

A very effective way to deepen this reflection is to invite someone you trust to participate in this analysis and share your results and self-perception with them. Show what you've learned about yourself, ask if they see any insights that you might not be seeing. A frank conversation can be powerful, and often the other person helps us identify our blind spots. When I, Susana, am teaching Personal Branding, I like to use the technique of putting people in pairs or trios to discuss their findings. It's very common for students to say that time was short. This happens because this discussion tends to be very deep and productive, with one person looking out for the other.

After analyzing the Johari Window, we suggest that you list some change actions that you can implement immediately, aligned with the insights you gained from your 360° feedback.

To arrive at these actions, think about how you could use this data to increase your success and personal fulfillment. How can your strengths add value to your Personal Brand? What changes do you need to make to minimize the points that could hinder you?

It's important to list actions and implement them right away. That way, you'll start moving your Personal Brand and aligning your mindset with your new attitude.

Mapping Your Brand DNA

When we started this process, you defined a goal, a place of recognition where you would like to be, and reflected on your Identity. Now let's connect all these points and anchor your goal in a broader vision of your life and what you want to build.

Now that you have a good idea of how your Personal Brand is perceived and know which talents are the foundation for your strengths, let's delve deeper into what you want to achieve by mapping your Brand DNA. It will be the foundation for consistent, authentic communication that comes from the heart. If you don't have this clear, you may feel a blockage in working on your Personal Brand, as happened with Cristiano, CEO of a beverage company, who reported the following difficulty: "I want to produce inspiring content, and I don't have time. However, no one I hire to help with this can write in a way that I feel represented."

Carolina, a marketing executive, approached us for the implementation of a brand ambassador program for the senior leadership of a pharmaceutical industry company. She brought us a complaint very similar to Cristiano's: "I've hired a press agency, a marketing agency, and even a freelancer to help us produce content for the group's executives. But it seems that no one can speak our language. They can't find our voice and produce content without soul."

This doesn't happen due to a lack of competence from content providers, but due to a lack of a larger strategic direction, one that isn't solely based on goals, but rather on meaning.

With DNA Mapping, the answers to the following questions will become clear:

- Why are we producing this content?

- What transformation do we want to generate in people?

- What long-term outcome do we want to leave for the world?

- What changes are made in the people we impact with our work if our plans come to fruition?

Furthermore, the answers form a unique and exclusive tie to your Personal Brand. There might even be someone who works in the same industry, with the same position and similar market objectives, but their personal motivations may be radically different. We're talking about values, vision, purpose, and flow state. They are the detailed components of your Personal Brand DNA, and just like genetic DNA, they may undergo some alterations over time, but they will continue to carry the essential information: who you are and what drives you.

Your Values

Our values define our behavior. According to coach Tony Robbins, values guide the person we want to be, influencing how we treat others and how we interact. Therefore, they determine who we are and how we interact with the world around us. Values are influenced by the experiences we have and the people around us. Robbins also emphasizes that values can change over time as our experiences and priorities change. Therefore, he encourages people to regularly assess their values and adjust them as needed to ensure they are always aligned with their goals and life purposes.

Use your values as guides to make decisions and lead your life according to your purposes and goals.

Your values were formed from your experiences, both personal and professional, people you interact with, and the surrounding environment. They tremendously impact the Personal Brand. For example, if security is a value for someone, they're constantly seeking to relate to trustworthy people, make secure investments, and plan their actions to avoid being surprised by their consequences.

To recognize your values, we propose a practical activity. We don't want you to make a list with beautiful words, but to think pragmatically. Value is what you truly hold in high esteem. In practice, it's where we put our time, resources, and energy. If you want to know what someone values, look at how they invest their most valuable assets - their time and money. Also, see how their schedule looks and where they allocate their resources.

Means value Vs. End value

It's very common for people to reflect as Malu does: "Oh, most of the time I spend working, but that's because what I value most is my family, and I work hard to ensure a good life for them." Therefore, it's important to make a distinction between what are means-values and what are end-values.

End values are abstract and represent deeper emotional states, reflecting what we desire for ourselves and what brings us fulfillment.

Means-values are ways to achieve our end-values.

For Malu, the end value is what she believes her family provides her: it could be love, intimacy, and security. Note that "family" may signify different emotional rewards, depending on what "family" means to each person.

" ACCORDING TO COACH TONY ROBBINS, VALUES GUIDE THE PERSON WE WANT TO BE, INFLUENCING HOW WE TREAT OTHERS AND HOW WE INTERACT."

In Malu's case, the financial reward from work is her way of nurturing her end value, which is family. Therefore, work and money are her means-values. She may say that she values it tremendously and even sacrifices family moments for her work because mentally, she's doing it to prioritize her higher value.

Practical Exercise

Evaluate the list below and reflect sincerely on what your values are, in order of priority. If you don't find any relevant value for you on the list, add it. The list of values is extensive, and some people prefer, for example, to say "stability" instead of "security". The important thing is that the word represents your feeling.

- Love/Affection
- Adventure
- Well-being
- Comfort
- Achievement
- Spirituality
- Generosity
- Hedonism
- Freedom
- Intimacy
- Power
- Passion/Emotion

- Recognition

- Health

- Security

- Success

Revisit your goal once again and assess if it is directed towards a means-value or an end-value. Often, short-term Personal Branding goals are related to means-values, while vision and purpose are related to end-values. There's no right or wrong here. The intention is not for you to change anything, only to identify and take ownership of what motivates you. The more you know yourself and understand where your inspiration comes from, the more strength you have to pursue your goals.

Recognizing what lies behind your desire for your Personal Brand, it will be easier to make course corrections if necessary. You may also eventually want to change your goal or switch a means-value to preserve what you seek as an end-value.

Otávio is an executive who had a difficult childhood and serious financial problems early in his entrepreneurial life. This environment made "security" a foundational end-value for him. However, today, Otávio is already a successful entrepreneur who has accumulated significant wealth. Nevertheless, he remains quite conservative in his decisions due to his history. The impact on his Personal Brand is that he ends up missing out on partnership opportunities due to his caution. Otávio could benefit greatly from greater visibility in networking groups with other entrepreneurs, where he could exchange experiences and bring innovative ideas to his business.

Despite having this desire, his natural tendency is to remain reserved. If Otávio does not recognize the origin of his motivation, he may both be criticized and harshly criticize himself for not exhibiting a certain type of behavior. He may want to work on his Personal Brand in networking groups but feel some sort of barrier to doing so. The exercise we recommend to him as the first step is to review which values are a priority.

When we become aware of the value that guides our actions, it becomes easier to identify how our daily behaviors are connected to the satisfaction of these values - and we can start to actively act to modify them. This doesn't mean that Otávio won't care about security anymore. It means that he has already achieved quite a satisfactory level of security, being able to stop being a hostage to an experience and start being guided by new values that make more sense with his goal. Each person can establish their strategy for this change in mental paradigm or seek the help of specialized professionals.

If you still have doubts about how to identify which values you prioritize, this tip may help: we know that something is a value for us when it is violated. Think about moments when you felt deeply offended by a person or situation: there lies something that is a value for you.

Values are non-negotiable elements. You have probably thought about this at some point in your life. So, now is the time to review them because they set the boundaries of your Personal Branding and define your territory of action.

Personal Vision

If vision is what you see ahead of you, Personal Vision is what you want to see happen, what you would like to happen, how you would like the world to be... all this considering your area of expertise! It is the definition of what you believe is possible to achieve or transform within your professional field. It is very important that this aspiration is related to what you do. In a 2022 McKinsey survey, 70% of professionals interviewed revealed that their sense of personal purpose is defined by their work. This is not for nothing. Our work is an important part of our Identity, and the closer it is to what brings us meaning, the greater the chance of success and happiness. Organizational psychologist Adam Grant once said, "The antidote to burnout may not necessarily be less work. It may be having more meaning."

Therefore, take some time to reflect on your vision. It can be something you achieve alone or a contribution you want to make to build something bigger, but it is a great desire that motivates you. This applies both to your current activity and to a future area you wish to migrate to.

> **" THE ANTIDOTE TO BURNOUT MAY NOT NECESSARILY BE LESS WORK. IT MAY BE HAVING MORE MEANING."**
>
> Adam Grant

Practical Exercise

We propose the following reflections:

- If I do what I propose for many years, what will be changed in the world?

- Within the environment in which I operate, in my professional arena, what legacy will I leave if I achieve my goals?

- Is this what I would like to see as a result of my professional activity?

If you think your Personal Vision is too abstract, think about a problem you could solve or an area you can transform or improve. Don't worry about writing a text to impact others. It's enough that the Personal Vision makes sense to you. Moreover, it can - and should - have emotion. Usually, when we write our Personal Vision, it comes from the heart. In summary, your Vision is the legacy you want to leave behind.

Personal Purpose

With your defined Personal Vision statement, it becomes more natural to think about your Purpose. Some people may call Purpose a mission, and there's no problem with that because the concept is what matters.

There is currently an avalanche of self-help advice which aims to solve in one impactful sentence, the difficult question of working in alignment with your purpose. And it's common to encounter people disappointed with themselves for not believing that their actions have a noble purpose since they don't directly work in the third sector or promote socially impactful actions.

However, in Personal Branding, Purpose is what you already do and will do to realize your Personal Vision. How will you act in the world to promote the realization of your vision? What do you literally "propose" to do to make your vision happen, even if it's only in that part of the world that you can impact? That's your Purpose. That's your Mission.

See how Personal Vision and Personal Purpose relate to these examples:

The Personal Vision of Naná Feller, a communication and collaborative processes professional, is "Sharing is caring." This is what she wants to see happening in the world.

Now, the Personal Purpose is the contribution she proposes to make: "to ensure that every project she participates in or leads has a representative from a group with marginalized rights."

On the other hand, Karina Lima, an experienced executive in "big techs," has always exercised very humanized leadership, encouraging her team to find personal meaning in their work. Her Personal Vision is a reflection of this way of thinking: "Expand the concept of customer success to all relationships, whether professional, personal, or philanthropic. I don't believe in B2B and B2C. We are one being and speak from people to people. When we connect our work with our values, merging brain and heart, we find high performance with purpose and create relationships where everyone wins: people, companies, and society."

Karina's Personal Purpose, or what she proposes to do to bring the world closer to this Vision is: "To practice high performance with purpose, connecting traditional success indicators to philanthropic and well-being practices. Promote environments where people can perform at their best potential, aiming for their success, their client's success, and the causes they connect with."

A vision doesn't need to have a long text to be profound. Look at the example of Fátima Pessoa, a fitness trainer.

- **Personal Vision:** "Feeling pain should not be normalized."
- **Personal Purpose:** "I work so that people can practice the sports they love, in the best physical condition possible, and with the least amount of pain."

Practical Exercise

Some questions to think about your Purpose:

- How can you contribute to the realization of your Personal Vision? What can you do to make what you want to happen in the world become a reality?
- If you manage to do what you propose to do in your work, what is the impact?
- As you put your talent in the service of the world, how much closer does the world get to your Personal Vision?

Look again at the goal you outlined in Chapter 5. And evaluate if it is aligned with your Personal Vision and your Personal Purpose.

State of Flow

When working on your Personal Brand, many people aim to literally follow almost a mantra, "love what you do, do what you love." What we love are the activities, interests, or topics that fascinate, motivate, and energize us. They make us jump out of bed early excited or engage in enthusiastic conversations for hours. Doing what you love is seeking happiness through work, attitudes, and hobbies. To identify how this happens in practice, you need to enter a state of optimal consciousness called flow.

The definition of flow was developed by Mihaly Csikszentmihalyi and characterizes the moment when a person is so engaged in what they are doing that nothing else matters. We reach a degree of concentration so great that we forget about other problems. The sense of time becomes distorted, either passing very quickly or very slowly. You enter a state of immersion so profound that your mind cannot focus on anything else. This is the state of flow.

It's no wonder that Mihaly is one of the leading thinkers of positive psychology. And this concept is intrinsically linked to what we discussed about talents. The more your Personal Branding goal is aligned with something that puts you in a state of flow, the greater your chance of success. What you are doing cannot be so challenging (i.e., distant from your talents) that it generates a state of anxiety, nor so easy for your skills that it instills a feeling of boredom.

When you place yourself between these two extremes, you can develop great pleasure in challenging yourself, surpassing yourself, and going a little further in this process each time. With this, you become better and better at what you set out to do. In Csikszentmihalyi's words: "The best moments of our lives are not the passive, receptive, and relaxing moments. The best moments usually occur when a person's body or mind is stretched to its limits in a voluntary effort to accomplish something difficult and worthwhile." It becomes clear, therefore, that doing what you love is less about liking or not liking something and more about the natural competence we have to do something extraordinarily well, and that brings us recognition for it.

Practical Exercise

Identify the professional situations in which you identify that the eight characteristics of flow described by Csikszentmihalyi occur:

- Complete concentration on the activity
- Clear goals and immediate feedback feeling
- Time distortion (acceleration/slowing down)
- The experience is intrinsically rewarding
- Little effort and ease of execution
- There is a balance between challenge and skills
- Actions and awareness merge
- There is a feeling of control over the task.

Compare what you discovered with your Personal Branding goal. Is what you intend to do aligned with what you do best and has the potential to bring you happiness?

Consolidating Your Identity

It's time to bring together everything you've reflected on about yourself. To organize so many ideas in a simple way that at the same time covers all the depth you've gone through, we suggest a tool called the Golden Circle. It became popular when in 2009, Simon Sinek brilliantly organized Identity like this:

- **Our Actions** = WHAT we do, what we concretely put into the world.

- **Our Way of Being** = HOW we do it, the way we establish relationships, our particular way of being and interacting in the world.

- **Our Vision** = WHY we do it, what moves us, our values, the way we see the world.

This model is based on anthroposophy, a discipline created by Rudolf Steiner, which consolidated knowledge of these three perspectives from diverse cultures and organized what he called "The 3 dimensions of Identity", which complement each other in an integrated manner. "Walking" through this circle brings us very interesting insights about ourselves.

Let's start by evaluating how tangible these dimensions are. Starting from the outside in, we realize that the further outside, the more tangible and concrete our actions tend to be. It is generally easier to describe WHAT we do. Isadora is an executive and leads a marketing team. Alberto is an endocrinologist doctor and sees patients in his clinic. Carolina is a developer and writes software.

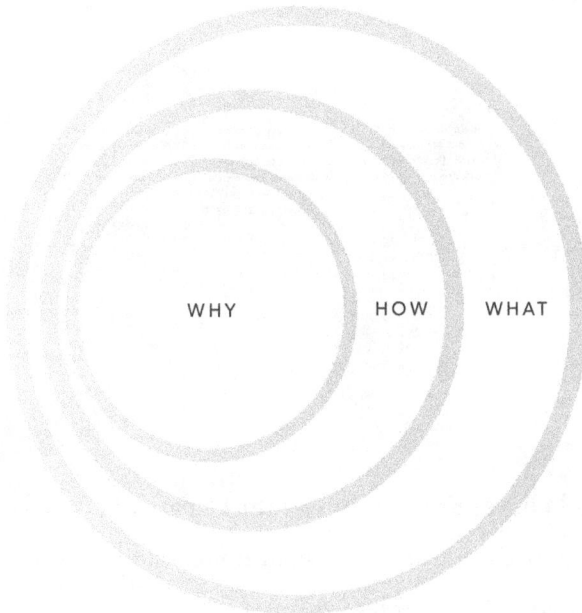

WHY   HOW   WHAT

When we move to the HOW, it becomes a bit more intangible. Isadora is organized and disciplined. Alberto is quite technical while being humane. Carolina is detail-oriented and careful. Note that in the HOW dimension, we can still see and perceive.

When we move to the WHY dimension, we enter the field of what is completely intangible, and we begin to deduce from what we see and feel. In the three examples, the essential value behind the professionals' actions is "respect." But for each of them, this value manifests itself in a particular way, which unfolds in their ways of acting:

Isadora believes that organization is a way to respect others' time and work. Therefore, her Golden Circle is like this:

Isadora

WHY	HOW	WHAT
Organization is a form of respect for people, as it ensures that their time and work are not wasted.	She is organized and disciplined. She establishes routines, demands discipline, and meets deadlines.	She leads a marketing team that develops innovative products for the company she works for.

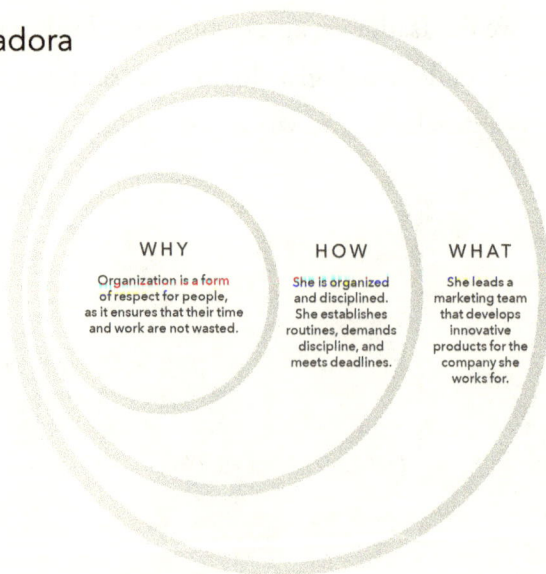

Alberto believes that a way to respect patients is only to proceed with scientific basis, but helping them understand what is being done. Hence his Golden Circle is like this:

Alberto

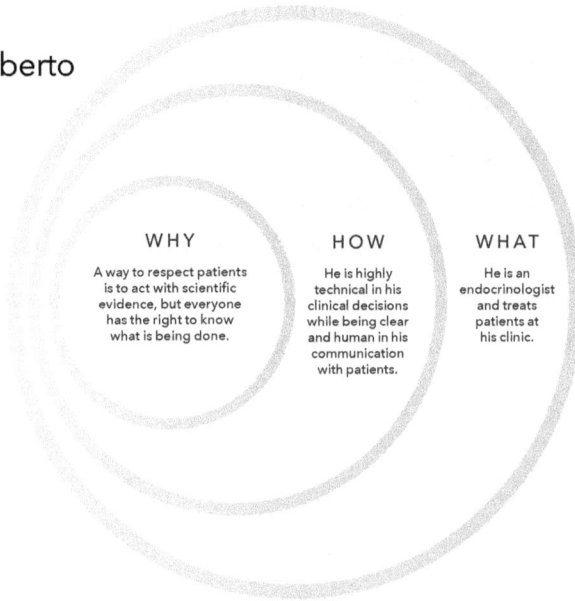

WHY

A way to respect patients is to act with scientific evidence, but everyone has the right to know what is being done.

HOW

He is highly technical in his clinical decisions while being clear and human in his communication with patients.

WHAT

He is an endocrinologist and treats patients at his clinic.

Carolina, who, in turn, has a strong sense of responsibility for her work in respect to those who hire her, had a Golden Circle like this:

Carolina

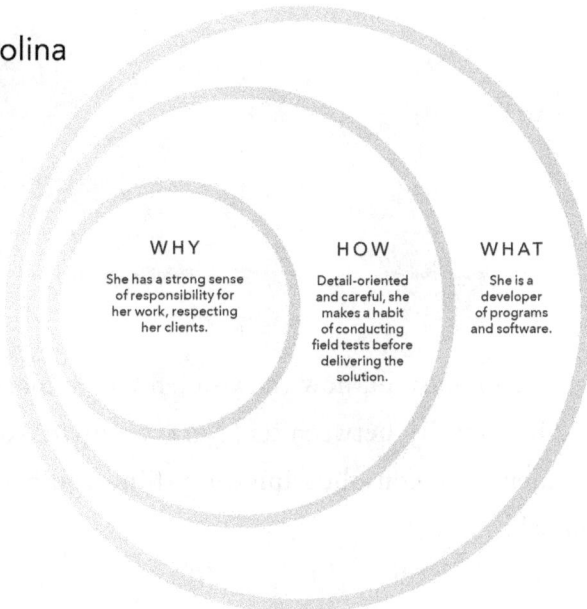

WHY

She has a strong sense of responsibility for her work, respecting her clients.

HOW

Detail-oriented and careful, she makes a habit of conducting field tests before delivering the solution.

WHAT

She is a developer of programs and software.

Now let's evaluate this tool in terms of flexibility. On the outer layer, where our actions are, we tend to be more flexible. WHAT we do in our daily lives can vary more easily. HOW we do it can also vary, but less. When it comes to WHY we do it, our deepest beliefs tend to be more stable over time. It is much easier to change what we do than to change what we believe. We don't change our beliefs overnight. For this reason, the outer dimension tends to be more flexible, variable, and the inner dimension, more stable and consistent.

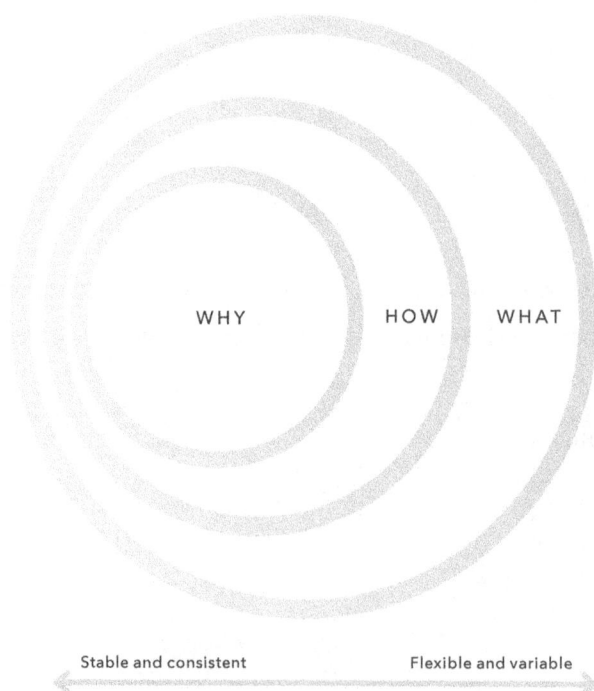

WHY   HOW WHAT

Stable and consistent   Flexible and variable

Now that you understand how the Golden Circle tool works and the difference in intensity between its layers, we invite you to fill in these three dimensions, consolidating everything you have reflected on about yourself.

You might think, "Wow, that's a lot! How am I going to put so many insights into such a small structure?" That is the idea. We want you to synthesize the information and be able to organize everything you've delved into about yourself into a simple structure. Imagine you're introducing yourself to someone and need to find a direct and powerful way to show who you are. Take a look at Noeli's, a lawyer, example:

- **What do you do?** Answer in a specific and concrete manner.

  "I'm a tax attorney specializing in family succession, working at a boutique law firm."

- **How do you do it?** Find your differentiators in what people said in your 360° feedback.

  "I'm always studying and improving. But I also invest time in getting to know my clients deeply. I consider their problems as my own. They feel my commitment, both technically and personally, and that's why they recommend me to their friends."

- **Why do you do it?** Recall your vision and purpose.

  "I believe that good succession planning is an act of love for those who remain. Death is a taboo, but we need to talk about it to ensure family harmony and the continuity of wealth."

Many people who believe they have no differentiation as professionals may be seeking their uniqueness in the answer to WHAT they do. However, oftentimes what we do can be quickly copied by someone else. And that's okay. In fact, this is something pioneers often struggle with. Usually, we differentiate ourselves by HOW we do it. By that particular, singular way that relates to your Identity, your repertoire, and your values. And the basis of our HOW usually comes from our WHY - what drives us to do what we do, the way we do it.

Now you can understand why this deep investigation leads to discovering powerful differentiators for your career and your life.

Finding this uniqueness is one of the secrets to strengthening a Personal Brand.

Practical exercise to conclude your Brand DNA

Fill in your Golden Circle by answering the following questions:

• What do you do?

Answer specifically and concretely, and remember to check if the activity you describe puts you in a state of flow.

• How do you do it?

Find your differentiators in what people said in your 360° Feedback and focus on the points that are most unique about your way of doing things and, therefore, more difficult to copy.

• Why do you do it?

Recall your Vision, Purpose, and Values.

I had the pleasure of meeting Giu and working with her during a very significant moment in my life, both personally and professionally. I was going through an important transition, leaving a position at a renowned clinic in São Paulo to pursue my dream of opening my own clinic, which today bears my name: Clínica Patricia Mafra.

Throughout this process, developing my Personal Brand was essential. Giu helped me recognize and reconnect with my values, my life purpose, and strengthen not only my name but also my identity in the world and the difference I can make in people's lives, especially my patients. She was crucial at every stage of this change and in the realization of my dream.

Working on Personal Branding is important for all of us, and Giu was the one who initiated this journey, helping me build this dream within my field of dermatology, which has always been my passion and life's purpose. Building my clinic and strengthening my Personal Brand were achievements made possible thanks to Giu's essential support throughout the process.

Dr. Patrícia Mafra,
Dermatologist - Founder of Clínica Patrícia Mafra

A STORY

"The Personal Branding process with Betafly was decisive for me to clearly identify my positioning. From there, when we organized my narrative, I was able to expand my presence and visibility with the key stakeholders in a market completely new to me, and I already see the results."

Cintia Capasso Co-Founder - Wecap Tech
Pediatric Audiologist - Stanford Children's Health Hospital

When Cintia Capasso approached us, she already had clarity about what her next career step would be: she wanted to leave one of the world's largest hospitals, Stanford, and become an entrepreneur. She had already reached the highest level at that hospital in her field of Neonatal Audiology. She liked her work, felt fulfilled, but understood it was time to think about the next step in her career.

When she encountered the Foldscope, a low-cost microscope made of paper with reusable slides, at a science fair at Stanford, a lightbulb went off. She saw an opportunity to represent the product in Brazil, bringing it into schools and stimulating children's interest in science. This process would be slow and parallel at first because she couldn't give up her job for the passion of the business. Cintia always believed in the product and the benefits it brings to its audience, but her greatest concern was how to enter the education market without having experience and proven involvement in this area.

HER CHALLENGES?

Cintia needed to find the guiding thread to tell her entrepreneurial story in a new market with credibility and confidence. Initially, she couldn't find a connection between her over ten years of experience as a neonatal audiologist and the education market in Brazil. Our perspective was that we needed to find a way to highlight all of Cintia's life and professional experiences to strengthen her brand with credibility in a new market. It remained to identify which "part" of her experience would bring value to her new professional movement. How to tie it all together and have an authentic narrative to generate a bond of trust with the new audience in schools? How to manage her networking to support her in this new journey?

THE PERSONAL BRANDING PROCESS

Our journey began with a retrospective of Cintia's trajectory up to the present moment and future expectations. In the 360° Feedback, it became evident that she is an entrepreneurial and visionary woman, extremely dedicated and committed to results. But it was only in the middle of the process, at one of the meetings in the Positioning stage, that she mentioned her first professional experience was as a teacher.

We then identified that throughout her professional journey, she had always been connected to education. After all, her experience of over twenty years as a pediatric audiologist involved developing emotional language with children. From there, we pulled the guiding thread to start building her narrative. A Brazilian doctor living in Silicon Valley who brought innovation to Brazilian schools through a product that stimulates students' interest and curiosity in science.

Cintia began to outline her future plan and connections she should make with teachers who would be her main allies in this new phase. She developed a training project for them to learn how to use the Foldscope. In addition to making connections with her networking in virtual and face-to-face meetings presenting her new pitch, she increased her visibility on social media. Throughout the process, she was even invited to be the CEO of a technology company, but she thought it best not to accept. Being a CEO was not in her plans. And the Personal Branding journey also brings more clarity about what not to do, to focus on her choices to take control of her own story, without being distracted by the "temptations" that arise along our journey.

CINTIA'S RESULTS

Tita, as we affectionately call her, continues with her project nd currently dedicates part of her time to expanding her business in Brazil. Her project has already impacted over 400 children in 8 schools, which had never seen a microscope. Afterwards, 70% said they were capable of conducting experiments independently without the teacher's assistance. This is just the beginning. Tita is still far from what she wants to achieve, but undoubtedly, her achieved numbers and the credibility she has been gaining in this new market already make her a great success story.

CHAPTER 8

POSITIONING

Up to this point, we've invited you to peel back your internal "layers," look within, and get closer to your essence in order to have a clear understanding of your Brand's DNA. This journey, which begins internally, from your inspirations and aspirations, now evolves into positioning your brand within your professional ecosystem literally.

Positioning is the space your Personal Brand occupies in people's minds as a memory that becomes associated with your name. Like in any ecosystem, there are various players (actors) simultaneously acting – for and against your brand.

In this second stage, we propose that you answer the question: "What do you want your name to be remembered, recognized, chosen, recommended for?", by taking the opposite approach. Instead of looking inward, look outward, look at the market, go to the arena, and understand what role your Personal Brand plays in the context it's in. Also, try to understand, primarily, what value you generate for the audiences that interact with you – your stakeholders.

Look at your audiences

What needs to be more evident in your Personal Brand is not about you, but how you serve your audience. The beauty of a strong Personal Brand happens when your talent meets a need, and you understand that what you do exceptionally well meets a deep need of a person or group of people. We can make an analogy: imagine two people dancing. The performance only becomes harmonious when both move in an integrated manner, without dominance, but with complementarity. When we create value for our audience, the perception of our Personal Brand's value increases. The client is satisfied and will likely recommend your service, increasing reputation and results, whether financial, emotional, relational, or of any nature. By dedicating yourself to making someone's life better, by helping them achieve something, your brand becomes necessary, desired, remembered, recommended. That is the essence of a strong Personal Brand.

To support you in this reflection practically, we use the 3 Ps of Positioning:

a) **Your Publics:** knowing who you create value for.

b) **Problem that annoys:** difficulty this audience faces, or ambition, something it aspires to.

c) **Promise of solution:** what you have to offer that solves the problem or what transformation helps promote.

Let's look at each of these Ps:

a) Your Publics

To structure your Positioning, the most important key turn is defining the audience you want to interact with. We always suggest choosing two or three different audiences that are positively impacted – truly benefited – by your achievements.

These people can be clients, your patients, partners, peers, people from your team, opinion leaders in the segment you operate in, participants in civil society organizations, government employees related to your field of activity, regulatory bodies of your professional class, influencers... the list is enormous. Because there's more than one, we'll refer to them as "your publics" instead of "your public".

They are your main stakeholders.

Practical Exercise: Develop a list of your main publics

Try to include groups with diversified relationships with your Brand. Important: do not include too many different publics to avoid losing focus and end up not effectively addressing anyone. Some criteria suggestions for your list:

- Strategic People / Necessary for your business: clients, agents;
- People who regulate your market or shape opinion: organizations, institutions;
- People who influence you or are influenced by you;
- People who depend on you: employees, suppliers;
- People who inspire and lead the segment in which you operate.

For your selection, you can think of a specific person you already relate to. For example, if you hold an executive position, this audience could be the manager of an area you serve in the company or want to serve. Or think of new clients who might be interested in what you do or have the potential to benefit from your delivery.

b) Problem that annoys

Now it's time to "put yourself in the shoes" of your audience and think how each person always has a goal, or set of goals, they are focused on to achieve an objective. We call this the "Job to be Done" - what your audience wants or needs to do to be successful. So, reflect: why do these people engage with you? Why do they seek you out? What makes you interesting to these people? What problem of your stakeholder do you solve, what do you do that improves this person's life?

To get the answers, we apply a tool created by Dave Gray, founder of XPLANE, called the Empathy Map. This map is widely used in Design Thinking processes. It's a methodology that originated here in Silicon Valley, in Palo Alto, California, where I, Giuliana, live. IDEO was the first company to use the DT approach in its projects to solve problems in a highly collaborative and interdisciplinary way. Most often, it involves professionals from different fields, such as design, technology, psychology, marketing, health, business... With this diversity, it's believed that there's an increase in the possibility of innovating on complex problems. Because of its success, other companies and organizations started to draw inspiration from it and use the approach in various sectors. Since then, DT has become a very popular methodology for innovation and entrepreneurship.

The design thinking process is divided into five major steps, and the empathic look at the audience is the first of them. Empathy is the ability to have curiosity and compassion for others, to seek to understand their motivations, aspirations, pains. All of this with the goal of truly understanding and sharing the feelings of another person. It's the ability to put yourself in someone else's shoes, trying to understand their thoughts, emotions, and perspectives, without judgment or criticism. Jesse Prinz, a philosophy professor at the City University of New York, Graduate Center, writes: "... sympathy is a third-person emotional response, while empathy involves putting oneself in someone else's shoes."

For this, an active process of listening and observation is necessary. Being empathetic allows you to better connect with your audience and strengthen your Personal Brand. When you show that you understand their pains, emotions, and desires, they are more likely to trust you and establish an emotional connection.

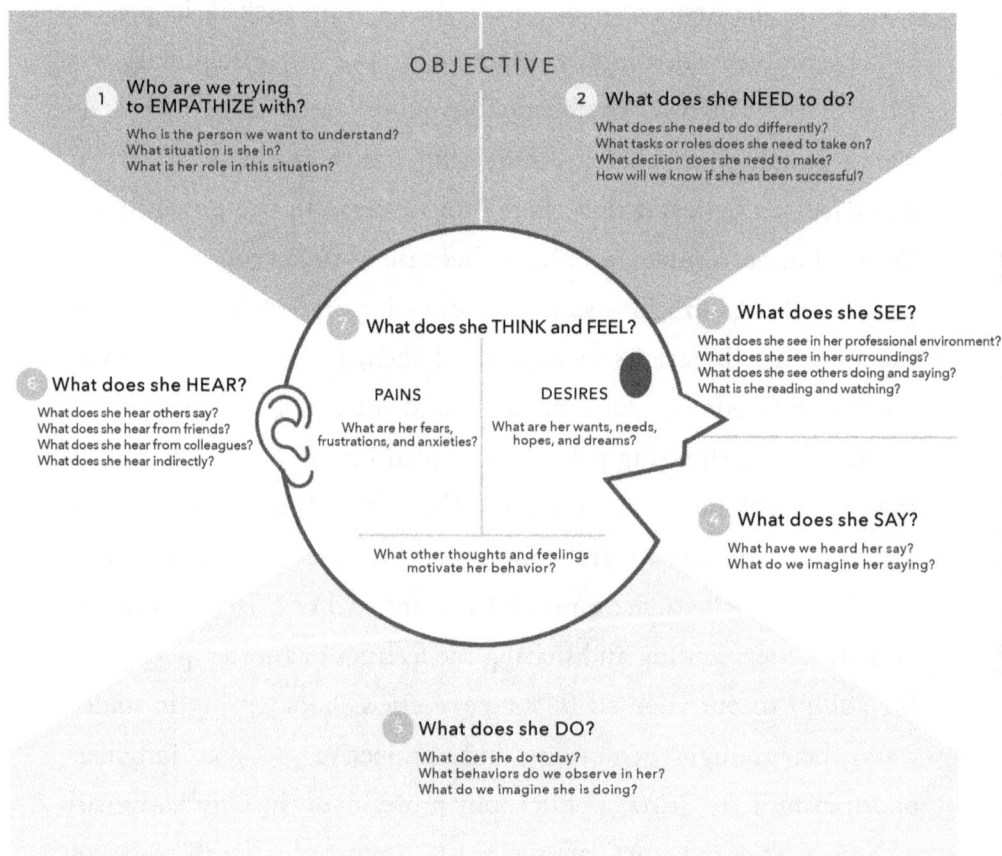

OBJECTIVE

1 Who are we trying to EMPATHIZE with?

Who is the person we want to understand?
What situation is she in?
What is her role in this situation?

2 What does she NEED to do?

What does she need to do differently?
What tasks or roles does she need to take on?
What decision does she need to make?
How will we know if she has been successful?

7 What does she THINK and FEEL?

3 What does she SEE?

What does she see in her professional environment?
What does she see in her surroundings?
What does she see others doing and saying?
What is she reading and watching?

6 What does she HEAR?

What does she hear others say?
What does she hear from friends?
What does she hear from colleagues?
What does she hear indirectly?

PAINS

What are her fears, frustrations, and anxieties?

DESIRES

What are her wants, needs, hopes, and dreams?

What other thoughts and feelings motivate her behavior?

4 What does she SAY?

What have we heard her say?
What do we imagine her saying?

5 What does she DO?

What does she do today?
What behaviors do we observe in her?
What do we imagine she is doing?

Practical Exercise

To fill out the empathy map, you can interview people who are part of your audience, or reflect only on what you know about them, but always try to put yourself in their shoes.

Questions to ask:

- **What does your audience think and feel?** Try to understand the main motivations, fears, desires, and needs of the target audience.

- **What does your audience see?** Consider the main points of contact that the target audience has with you or some other point of contact with your brand that is not necessarily through you.

- **What does your audience hear?** Think about the main communication channels that your audience uses and the messages they are receiving.

- **What does your audience say and do?** Consider the behavior and actions of your audience, as well as the things they say about your Personal Brand.

- **What are the main pains and gains of your audience?** Identify the main needs, challenges, and benefits that your audience seeks.

Once the map is completed, you will have a deeper understanding of your audience and be better able to offer more relevant and attractive products, services, and content. This can help differentiate your Personal Brand from the competition and increase your relevance in the market.

a) Promise of result

The secret to good Positioning is the match between what you offer and what your audience needs - the famous "stomach ache" that they need to solve. This is the foundation for building a Personal Brand with a defined Positioning. A person is hired because they do a job that their client can't do alone. We go to a restaurant because we want an experience that we can't reproduce in our own home. We buy clothes because they give us a specific performance, a status attribute that we don't have without them.

After identifying the problem that people seek to solve with you, develop the Value Promise of your Personal Brand.

Practical Exercise

Thinking that all the people who are part of these audiences have their challenges, desires, ambitions, obstacles, answer: what is a problem of theirs that you can solve? What do you do that improves these people's lives?

Think about everything you offer: experience, value, differentiators, and, especially, the result they will have. Also reflect on how you do it differently from other people, even those who work in the same activity.

The following questions can help in this exercise:

- What do you do – objectively?

- How do you do it? (drawing from your feedback – what your audiences point out as your "way")

- What do you do differently / uniquely?

- What impact do you have on your audiences?

- What results do your audiences experience?

- What changes in their lives, practically speaking? What transformation do you promote?

Looking at the environment

The goal of analyzing the environment in which your brand operates is to help you understand your real position in this big chessboard called the "market." Whether it's favorable or unfavorable, whether there are many or few competitors, whether there are many products or services similar to yours.

We serve professionals from various fields, such as executives, entrepreneurs, and freelancers like lawyers and doctors. Until recently, these professionals didn't worry much about their positioning in the market. In some cases, they couldn't even engage in any marketing activities because regulations in their own segment prevented them. But the market has changed and has been pressuring these organizations to evolve according to demand. As a result, we see professionals from all areas learning terms that were previously restricted to marketing professionals, such as 'differentiation.'

We all have something that makes us unique, the Brand DNA. Yet, when looking at the market, we might feel like we're doing more of the same when compared to colleagues in the same field. For example, dermatologists. At first glance, it may seem like there's no differentiation, that everyone does exactly the same thing. So, how can we help a dermatologist identify their differentiation if they offer the same service as many others? Well, if there were no difference, there wouldn't be doctors much more sought after than others. Even offering something that may seem similar, such as technologies and raw materials available in the market to everyone, it's possible to highlight the Personal Brand's differentiation of each one.

Each dermatologist comes with a completely different life baggage, experience, connections, learnings. Even though they offer the same service, each one serves, delivers, prepares, and has a completely different post-treatment. Each one offers a unique patient journey. In other words, each doctor has their way of impacting with their brand, creating an experience that becomes a "registered trademark" in the patient's mind and generates connection. If they fail to generate any emotion or connection with their audience, then their service becomes a commodity. Without differentiation, the patient will seek the cheapest doctor. When a professional can identify their differentiation and make it visible, the patient will recognize their value and pay to experience that and get the best result. It's important to emphasize that technique is a prerequisite. Knowing how to do what you do well, being passionate about your profession isn't a differentiator, it's the minimum you can deliver. The question is: what else can you do and be to delight and surprise your patient?

The same logic applies to executives, lawyers, entrepreneurs... What is your differentiator, what set of skills makes you deliver something unique? It's within you. It's not useful to copy your colleague. It needs to be authentic because only then will you connect with your audience, and your audience will recognize your value, valuing your Personal Brand for it.

Practical Exercise: Investigate your professional segment

- **Who else does what I do - directly or indirectly - and how are these people positioning themselves?**

  Don't see only those who directly operate in the same market as your "competitors." Also, consider those who do analogous activities or compete for the attention, time, and resources of your audiences.

- **What do my competitors communicate?**

- **How do my competitors communicate?**

- **To whom do they communicate?**

- **What do they offer, and what image do they convey?**

Your differentiator is what will make you stand out from other colleagues, become more attractive to clients, and establish credibility in your market with a unique approach. We're talking about being memorable and remembered, meaning, generating emotion in your client. This is in your potential and human capabilities, which are your HOW, your way of doing and delivering your service or product. Differentiation helps you choose a unique Positioning, which will make your Personal Brand remembered and recognized. Comparing yourself can generate some insecurity at first, but undoubtedly, it broadens your perspective and leads to more business opportunities or for your career.

Looking at your inspirations

In addition to understanding the context in which your Personal Brand is currently positioned, aim for the future and where you want to go. One way to do this is to look at who serves as a reference for you. Not with the intention of imitating them, as this breaks the DNA of your brand and is not sustainable. The focus here is to draw lessons and open your eyes to interesting paths they tread. Models help us project who and how we want to be, and even how we "don't" want to be. In business projects, we call this benchmarking. Having your internal starting point is fundamental. But by looking outward, you refine your Value Proposition and find your path to authenticity. It's by interacting with others that your Identity happens in the world. Therefore, strategically mapping the environment in which your Personal Brand operates involves analyzing:

- people who do what you would like to do;

- people who are in places where you would like to be;

- people who simply inspire you for something they do, even if it's not everything.

Often, you pick inspiration from a specific thing someone does, an interesting aspect of another. Don't look for the perfect person. Don't look for the ideal model. Look for aspects that seem interesting to you and that you can learn from. This inspiration is precisely to understand how the spaces are filled in the market by colleagues or competitors and to define your space in this market in an authentic and unique way. When we talk about market positioning, we refer to the "position" you will occupy in the market. That's why this market analysis, this outward look, is fundamental and necessary.

Practical Exercise

- Make a list of the people who inspire you;

- Reflect and describe which aspects seem attractive to you and that can be adapted to your Personal Brand;

- Finally, evaluate if there's anything in common among your inspirations, and if you can draw any more insights from this reflection.

The answers obtained from this market analysis help to make the reality clearer. None of us lives in isolation: we are part of an ecosystem in which we interact, contribute, inspire, and learn.

Define the territory of your Personal Brand

To define your Positioning, you need to make choices. Some clients struggle with this task which may involve, for example, giving up a client portfolio, halting the offer of some services, and stopping work on a certain front. The struggle comes because the feeling is that you're leaving money on the table or refusing to deliver your service to someone. But trying to please everyone doesn't deliver value to anyone. And those who try to please everyone end up pleasing no one. It's what we call "plain vanilla," and there's a joke that says, *in Personal Branding, we shouldn't be vanilla ice cream.* Vanilla ice cream is tasty, but it's not something wonderful. It's not something that people generally love nor is it something that people generally hate. It's simply a great accompaniment to any other dessert that has personality. If you order a brownie, it might come with vanilla ice cream. If you order an apple pie a la mode, ditto. Because those without personality go with anything. But a salted caramel ice cream, well, that's different. It has a striking unique personality. Not everyone may like it. But some people will love it, and they will have an emotional connection with that flavor. Others will detest it, and that's okay too. The important thing is that it has a defined territory.

It seems incredible, but it's easier to choose what we want to do than to have the courage to say no to everything else outside of this square. So, to facilitate this choice process, we propose a change of vision here: giving up is not losing opportunities but making room in your schedule to attract exactly what you're willing to do according to what you can deliver best to your audience's needs.

We like to bring the approach of "essentialism," which focuses on seeking what is fundamental in our lives, eliminating what is unnecessary or superficial. Currently, we live in a world with a lot of noise and distractions. Therefore, applying the essentialism approach helps us eliminate what doesn't make sense, focusing and shedding light on what is most important and significant. Choosing the essential is increasing the perception of value of your brand and living more aligned with your values and goals.

In our experience with clients, after they manage to exercise detachment and define their Positioning, we hear testimonials like: "It's liberating to say no to what was filling my schedule and bring in what makes more sense for my current moment." This will be an important achievement because you will be able to do what you really always sought in a more structured way and with intention.

This is what happened to Giulia, co-CEO of a family company in the food industry. She founded and built the company alongside her husband. However, even though they share tasks and merits, the strong sexist burden still present in our society leads to a widespread perception that only he is the owner, and she is there in leadership, because she is his wife. Personal Branding work helped her identify her unique contribution to the business and thus define her area of action more clearly. Not with the intention of competing with her husband, but rather of collaborating (co-laboring = laboring together) for the company they both lead. This clarity of roles benefited not only Giulia herself, who began to see her leadership more clearly, but also the entire team working in the company. By better understanding the responsibilities and boundaries of each leader, work began to flow more efficiently.

Credentials to Support Your Positioning

"Pillars" are what we call all the experiences and life events that have led us to "know what we know." We could also call them "credentials" because, in a way, they are the basis of your credibility and support your position as a reference in your field of expertise.

It's from these that the audiences of your Personal Brand recognize your authority on the topics you address.

When reflecting on your Personal Brand, we recommend that you rescue these elements that support your Positioning. We've organized them into four categories, but feel free to add any other experiences that you believe qualify you:

Courses

This is what we most easily remember to mention and inquire about as credentials.

Experiences

These are all the experiences we've had that enrich us personally and professionally. They can be professional experiences, conferences, symposiums, projects, cultural trips, volunteering, sabbaticals, exchanges, expatriation, etc.

Skills

Everything we know how to do, by talent or learning, and that sets us apart. For example: aesthetic sense, sensitivity to human beings, teamwork, leadership, language skills, spatial vision, etc.

Intellectual Property

Many people answer "I don't have–" to this question because they usually associate this term with patents or publications. But we want you to expand this concept to any content you've developed for your business that has your personal touch, your perspective, or your approach.

It could be an adaptation of a service method, a different or exclusive way of providing a service, something you conceived in your field of expertise.

Think about what makes you different:

- Have you written or produced any documents in your field? Books, articles, lectures, or classes?

- Is there a model you created and use in your activity, even if you haven't documented it?

- Do you have a unique way of working, recognized by your clients? Something they tell you about the exclusive benefits they get when they buy your product/service?

Your Unique Value Proposition

After going through all the reflections, we suggest you define your Positioning where you will have identified your skills, knowledge, experiences, Identity, talents. All of this together is what makes you a unique person. Now, define what to highlight to become relevant to your audience. This will be your Unique Value Proposition.

You'll need to craft a one-paragraph text-- just one paragraph-- that synthesizes and organizes the value you generate. Always remembering that your Personal Brand is alive. Therefore, you can and should continuously review this Positioning. This will be a document just for you, internal and strategic. So feel comfortable expressing yourself in the most spontaneous and genuine way you want. The statement is the heart and soul of your Personal Brand and will serve as the basis for your communication from now on.

To create the text, think about your main achievements and the accomplishments you're proud of. Then, review your goals and the professional achievements you want to reach in your next cycle.

Structure it as follows: a description (I) of what you do; followed by (II) the impact you have on your audience by doing this, and (III) "seasoned" with what makes you different.

Here's an example: if I, Susana, think of what I offer to my audience as: "*I offer Personal Branding consulting,*" I would be focused only on the "process," of what I do. But those who buy "process" prioritize the lowest price because they don't recognize my value.

People buy "results," which we deliver through a "process," and that, indeed, has value.

So, rewriting my Positioning according to the structure of the Unique Value Proposition, I come up with this text:

"Using strategic thinking and powerful questions, I help executives and entrepreneurs organize their narrative for the market, from within themselves to the outside. Through an exclusive method of Personal Branding, developed by me and my partner, we apply our experience of over 20 years in corporate Branding. By becoming more visible, my clients increase their opportunities, job satisfaction, and engagement with their stakeholders." – Susana, Betafly.

Practical Exercise: Use this structure to guide you

Using my talent/method/experience (Differentiator) _____
_____,
I offer (My work) _____
through methodology/style/way (How) _____
_____ so that they can/are able to/achieve (Result/impact)
_____.

Using the same text, try reversing the order, putting the result for the client first and then explaining what you do and how you do it so that they achieve this result. See if it works better or not. There are various ways to combine these elements, find the one that works best for you.

Susana, I want to tell you that I started the BetaFly Program with you feeling a certain impatience and anxiety because at that moment I wanted a quick answer to make several professional decisions. The impatience came from having to provide 30 friends for you to interview, plus 20 clients!

I thought, "This work of interviewing 50 people is going to take over a year to show any results."

But, to my surprise, with each passing day, I received so much feedback, information, and comments that, almost just from the interviewees' testimonies, I already felt motivated to take the next steps.

And the benefit was almost immediate. Through our meetings, I was able to clearly identify my main skills, and more than that, understand how the outside world perceives me, which gave me the confidence to face challenges with much more security.

I learned a lot about my talents, and the way you conducted all the sessions helped me see myself and my place in the world more clearly. Not only that, it allowed me to focus on developing my strengths and, at the same time, gave me a clearer awareness of my weaknesses and limitations. The structure of your course helped me work on overcoming these challenges.

As a result, I felt more comfortable and confident in making decisions that I had previously delayed, and today I am committed to using this learning with great discipline in my work and communication as a whole.

Fernando Sálvia,
Board Member, Lawyer, and Tax Consultant

A STORY

> "Betafly's work was inspirational for me to expand my voice in order to fulfill my purpose, which is to help shape better people, contributing to a better world. And I believe that women have a fundamental role in this construction."

Thiago Coelho - CEO of Estrella Galicia Brewer

When we met Thiago, he had already been elected three times as the most inspirational leader of the year at Coca-Cola, where he had worked for 15 years and held the position of Vice President for Central America. His purpose of helping people to build a better world was almost crystal clear, and he spoke about it fluently. Those who knew him could clearly perceive, and still can, how truly motivated he is by this.

There was just one caveat: one had to talk to him, work with him, be close to him, to feel and perceive this. There was little content about Thiago in interviews, posts, and articles that were connected to his purpose. Our challenge to him was: "Searching for you in the media, in general, we can't see all this power and clarity of purpose that we're feeling here, live." That was enough for him, a quick and assertive person, to mobilize and start a Personal Branding process.

HIS CHALLENGES?

To make his motivations more explicit to people. What was interesting in Thiago's case was that the first stage of the FLY® Method about self-awareness, purpose, and future vision were already solved for him. That's why we agreed that we needed to act on communication.

THE PERSONAL BRANDING PROCESS

We decided to start the journey with the elaboration of the Golden Circle, which is part of the Brand DNA stage, in order to consolidate Thiago's Personal Brand identity. We used as a basis all the reflections he had made alone until then. What emerged was very interesting.

In Thiago's "Why," were:

- People are a living legacy;

- Women make the world better.

In his "How," he put:

- Closeness with people, understanding what drives them;

- Walk the Talk.

In his "What" there was:

- Ensuring delivery, creating value for stakeholders;

- Seeking and implementing business growth opportunities.

With the Identity organized in these 3 dimensions, we carried out the entire Communication stage so that his key messages, narratives, and all forms of expression contributed to making this construction clear in people's minds.

THIAGO'S RESULTS

Thiago left no more doubts about his convictions. His communication became more straightforward.

In 2023, already as CEO of Estrella Galicia brewery, and without ever letting go of the dynamic pace that his position and the business he leads demand, he reached 50 thousand followers on LinkedIn, was nominated for the best award as an HR influencer, and was invited to speak on the topic of female leadership in companies.

Thiago continues to be an inspirational leader, now not only recognized by the companies where he works, but also by so many people who connect with his concepts and ideals.

CHAPTER 9

PERSONAL BRAND
COMMUNICATION
STRATEGY

The foundation of a strong Personal Brand is delivering value to your audience - and communicating that is a necessary and powerful reinforcement, as it is our tool of connection with the world. As Matt Abrahams, a lecturer at Stanford Graduate School of Business, the author of *Think Faster, Talk Smarter: How to Speak Successfully When You're Put on the Spot* and *Speaking Up Without Freaking Out*, and the host of *Think Fast, Talk Smart ThePodcast*, said: "The ability to present your ideas clearly, confidently, and authentically can make a big difference in the success you will achieve in your professional (and personal) life."

There are a series of actions - online and offline - that can be taken to communicate your Personal Brand to your target audiences. By expressing your ideas and interacting strategically based on your Brand DNA and Positioning, you strengthen aspects of your reputation and build a perception of who you are aligned with your Unique Value Proposition. In this way, you make it clear in the minds and hearts of people what your role in the world is and how you can add value to their lives through it.

" THE ABILITY TO PRESENT YOUR IDEAS CLEARLY, CONFIDENTLY, AND AUTHENTICALLY CAN MAKE A BIG DIFFERENCE IN THE SUCCESS YOU WILL ACHIEVE IN YOUR PROFESSIONAL (AND PERSONAL) LIFE."

Matt Abrahams

Why communicate

We see people who, even with a well-built Unique Value Proposition, hesitate to communicate their Personal Brand out of insecurity, fear of criticism from competitors, or thinking that it is self-promotion. But with a Communication Strategy, everything you communicate will focus on building value for your brand. Here are some aspects you will work on:

Communicate to build reputation

Your reputation is one of your greatest assets: it literally works for you. This is because it is built from what others perceive from your words, actions, and presence. That is why the famous advertising executive David Ogilvy once said: "communication is not only about what you say, but mainly, about what the other person understands." Your reputation precedes you in the room and remains after you leave.

To have some influence in the formation of your reputation, you need to act consciously and attentively in emitting your message, thus increasing the chance that other people may perceive, as faithfully as possible, what you want to express.

To make the reputation of your Personal Brand easily understood, it is very important to define in which attributes you will shed more light, and then communicate them efficiently. This will make your projected image (what you emit, project to others) close to your perceived image (what the other person actually captures).

Put simply, the communication process works as follows:

1. The person emitting the communication decides the message they want to convey

2. The person emitting the communication decides how they will communicate their message: chooses words, uses certain body language, codes, or symbols

3. The person emitting the communication transmits the message and the receiver receives the message

4. The receiver translates this message into ideas

5. The receiver draws conclusions, and responds or not to the message

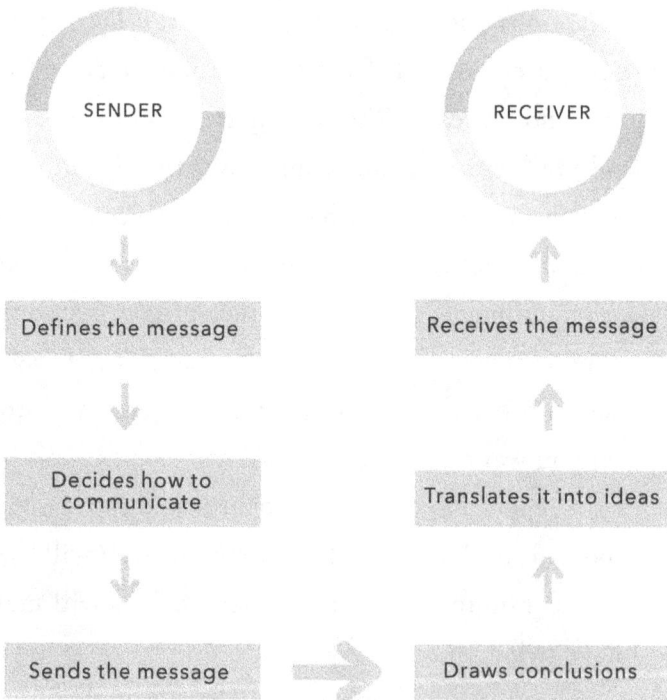

SENDER

RECEIVER

| Defines the message | Receives the message |

| Decides how to communicate | Translates it into ideas |

| Sends the message | Draws conclusions |

But a fun – and true – way to explain this process is:

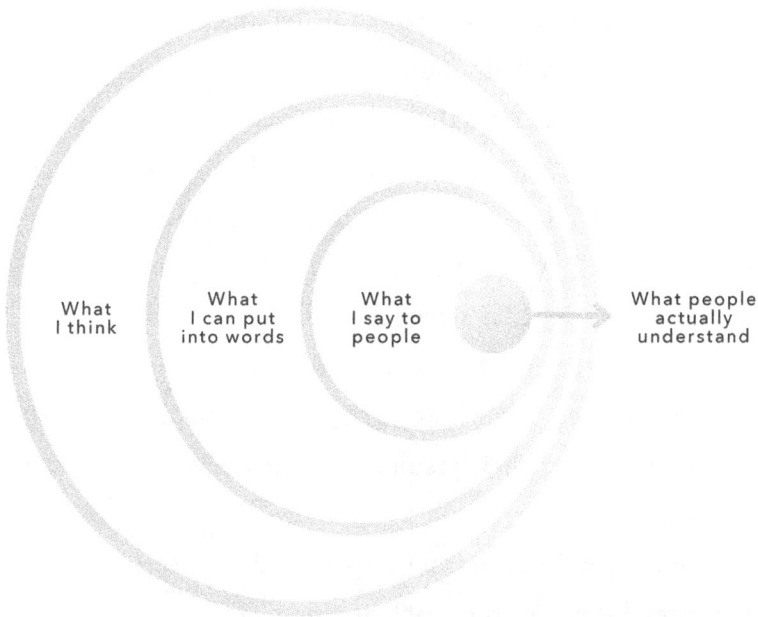

What
I think

What
I can put
into words

What
I say to
people

What people
actually
understand

Communicate to build credibility

Authority and credibility are two words that go hand in hand, but there is a subtle difference between them. Your authority is given by your skills, knowledge, and professional experience. Being an authority on a subject means having mastery over that topic. The credentials that attest to your authority are your value that needs to be communicated. As basic as it may seem, you need to show. People need to see to believe.

On the other hand, credibility is the result of this work of showing your credentials. It is conferred to you by your audience, who attribute credibility to your brand, recognizing that you are an authority on a certain subject. Many people want to have this recognition, but it is earned as you gain the trust of others. And how do you achieve this? Through communication, which is the link between everything you know and do, and your audiences.

A process that accelerates this recognition is the so-called "authority trigger." Mental triggers are stimuli that the brain recognizes and drives people to make decisions. In practice, these stimuli generate a response, especially when it comes to making a particular choice.

The authority trigger is strengthened when you demonstrate expertise in the subject to people in your field, sharing information about the market, data, business, and talking about success stories, number of clients and their results, recognized partners, awards received, and testimonials.

Let's say you read a professor's resume and discover that they have written successful books and teach at renowned universities. This increases your confidence in the quality of their teaching. Similarly, we tend to give more credit to what is told to us by a person in a white coat and not always ask them to show us a diploma to follow their guidance. We respect a traffic officer or a person wearing a robe. Through codes we have learned since childhood, our brains draw immediate conclusions about the reputation and authority of people.

You can use mental triggers to benefit your Personal Brand in various ways. For example, if you can find written content, videos, and references about your name in various places, this increases the chance that people will believe that you, having visibility with relevant content, must also be competent.

Therefore, we cannot emphasize enough: the obvious needs to be said.

We tend to get used to our own content. Dealing with the same topic every day for a long time, we end up thinking that certain information is obvious and everyone must already know it. This is not true. What may seem routine to you may not be so clear to others, and it can be transformative in someone else's life. The only chance for your content to positively impact someone is for you to take the initiative to express it to your audiences tirelessly.

The fear of communicating what seems obvious also comes from that place of impostor syndrome, that voice within us that makes us believe we are not good or capable enough.

Be careful: the fear of seeming trivial can paralyze the development of your Personal Brand. If you identify with this feeling, look around and observe how many professionals achieve great professional success by talking about topics that don't seem so complex. Don't be your worst critic. On the contrary, have a generous look at what you can offer to the world in the form of relevant content.

Moreover, we often believe that if we communicate something once, everyone already understands, memorizes, and moves on from the subject. But studies show that we remember, on average, only 10% of all the communication we receive. Therefore, communication is about repetition. The more we communicate about a point, the more we increase the chance of people retaining the message. And it is necessary to find creative ways to tell the same story in different ways and to use different narrative structures to convey your central messages.

Communicate to be chosen

One of the factors that makes a professional be chosen over others is the amount of positive information people have. This type of data triggers another mental trigger: social proof, which favors the choice of a particular person. Social proof is a psychological and social phenomenon. In his book *Influence: The Psychology of Persuasion*, psychology and marketing professor at Arizona State University, Robert Cialdini, described how people are influenced by the choices of others. It works like this: imagine a new aesthetic procedure being performed by various specialists. And one clinic has already successfully applied it to hundreds of clients. There is a tendency for people to feel more confident in undergoing the procedure at the clinic that has a track record of successful cases. This is because when we show significant adoption, we increase the chances of convincing someone that they are not embarking on an adventure, but on something that many have already proven to be effective.

We are not talking about simply being visible, but intentional visibility with strategy. It doesn't need to be mass communication with a large audience. The most important thing is that your audiences have access to information that triggers mental responses and increases the chances of being chosen by you.

What to communicate

Let's start building the backbone of your communication. Just as the spine supports our body, your key messages form an axis that you will use to ensure that your communication is clear and consistent. They make up a kind of editorial line of your brand. An editorial line gives guidance on what will be communicated through a medium. For example, you wouldn't expect to find fashion articles on a sports blog. That would be a surprise for readers who are looking for game results, match comments, or athlete profiles. It may seem like we are exaggerating, but some people vary their topics so much that they may even seem like a general news website.

Another point to consider is not to be a blind shotgun, wanting to suffocate your stakeholders with a million different points, details that are usually only relevant to you. Focus your awareness that less is more. Remember this: a strong Personal Brand is recognized for being specifically relevant in a particular area of expertise.

Another important aspect is defining the approach to your topics. Produce authentic, original content. When you do this, you convey your identity and build credibility. A tip: don't repeat content just for the sake of it, but try to provide your perspective on it. In addition to being original, also aim to be relevant. So, you saw a new and interesting topic in your field, read a news piece or an article that connects to your message? Reflect:

1. What is your opinion on that, considering all your knowledge and experiences in the sector? Share your thoughts.

2. Is it something of value to your audiences? Share it.

Original and valuable content builds authority and reinforces your credibility.

When choosing your content, also consider this reflection from Maytê Carvalho, author of the best-seller *Persuasion - A Practical Guide on Rhetoric and Persuasive Communication in Your Personal and Professional Life*: If all WhatsApp messages were public, what information about you would others know? What would they reveal about the person you are? This exercise is meant to help you extract genuine aspects of yourself and then work on them intentionally and in your favor.

Key Messages

Let's revisit the Personal Branding process of executive Alexandre Correa as he reflected on his Brand DNA, arriving at two words to define himself: intra-entrepreneur and ambidextrous. See how his brand's key messages turned out:

Key Message 1: How to build an innovation/new business structure in large corporations.

Developments:

- The Chief Entrepreneur's vision

- Innovation processes/tools

- Innovation return assessment

- Holistic view of the chain and its impact on innovation projects

- The new normal for R&D

- Global vs. local vision for project launches.

Key Message 2: B2B Sales.

Developments:

- Application of digital marketing for B2B sales

- B2B prospecting funnel and processes

- Value generation in B2B vs. B2C

- Construction of commercial, technical, and technical-commercial structures

- Challenges and opportunities

- Adjacent Topic 2: Service marketing

Key Message 3: : Startups in large corporations.

Developments:

- Cultural challenges of implementing a 'startup' team in traditional companies
- Nature vs. Nurture: challenges and opportunities of incorporating or leading new businesses by area
- Talent management in startups (resource pool, specialists, permanent vs. consultants)
- Internal marketing and how to keep innovation relevant
- Hero Product and pivoting

Another example is Mariana, an architect who works for a company known for launching innovative projects aligned with a more contemporary lifestyle. She believes that a home is much more than a place where we sleep and stay sheltered. Above all, it is an extension of ourselves. Her purpose is for every person, regardless of the size of the house or apartment they can afford, to have the opportunity to live in a place that represents their identity and is practical and functional as demanded by the current world.

Key Message 1: Design as an element that transforms lives.

Developments:

- Design trends in urban housing
- Sharing vs. ownership - why we don't need to own everything
- New building materials
- How to make the most of small spaces
- Smart decoration

Key Message 2: ESG in the construction industry.

Developments:

- Circular economy

- New building materials (Same subject addressed in theme 1, but here with a sustainability angle)

- Buying opportunities

- Training base professionals in the construction industry with art and aesthetics lessons.

Mariana chose two key messages that already fully express both what she does as a professional and what her purpose in her work is. These are the themes that we want to come to mind for your audiences when they think of your name. In Mariana's case, these are the themes that she should repeat for a sufficient period of time for her name to be remembered and associated with them - we suggest at least a year. Remember that repetition should bring content, conveying the same message in different ways. This way, she will ensure consistency in her communication.

Personal Themes

If you wish and feel comfortable sharing something more personal, we suggest creating a "snapshot" of your life that has a connection to your work, or that adds an attribute you want to build. This not only expands your content, but also brings your experience and connects with your audience, reinforcing your Personal Brand.

When communicating personal subjects, we suggest they be in context with the key messages you have already chosen. Inserting purely personal content, isolated, out of context, although having a good chance of attracting an audience, does not add as much value to your Personal Brand, and may even create a distraction for something that people interact with more out of curiosity than to reinforce your credibility.

Undoubtedly, personal themes connect you with your audience on a more human and accessible level, in addition to your professional attributes. As we have already mentioned, we do not like formulas, so you need to be comfortable with sharing a snapshot of your personal life. If it adds value to your Personal Brand, it is interesting to use this resource.

Our client Augusto, a senior executive in the construction industry, recognized for his work with over 20 years of experience, decided to use fatherhood as a personal theme. Showing himself as a dedicated and involved father, sharing stories from his experience helped humanize him and showcase his leadership skills that go beyond the corporate environment. Some posts he made on LinkedIn with this theme had a huge impact. And notice, Augusto used the personal theme to add value to his brand with intention and strategy. This made all the difference.

Practical Exercise

To define the key messages that can form the backbone of your brand, think about:

- Content on which you have knowledge and expertise to speak about.

- Content that interests your audiences and keeps them connected to you.

- Content that speaks about what drives you (your vision and purpose, which you developed in the DNA stage).

Now, choose one to three themes that will support the points above. Write a sentence about each of them that conceptualizes what that means to you.

We call these themes "umbrellas," because they cover everything. After defining each theme, write below how each of them unfolds into subthemes.

KEY MESSAGE 1 and its meaning for you:	KEY MESSAGE 2 and its meaning for you:	KEY MESSAGE 3 and its meaning for you:
Developments 1:	Developments 1:	Developments 1:
Developments 2:	Developments 2:	Developments 2:
Developments 3:	Developments 3:	Developments 3:
Developments 4:	Developments 4:	Developments 4:
Developments 5:	Developments 5:	Developments 5:

PERSONAL THEMES

Personal theme 1 and the context that will strengthen your Brand:

_____

_____

_____

Personal theme 2 and the context that will strengthen your Brand:

_____

_____

_____

Your Biography or Bio

It is important to have a base text that tells your story, which can serve various purposes in your professional life. This text, your Bio, is your story, told by you. It is very common to be asked for a Bio when you are going to participate in an event, publish something, or even for your social networks. Having a base text, your Bio can be expanded into smaller versions ("mini bios") to be used in lectures, classes, at the end of articles you write, or on any other occasion. In each situation, you can choose to highlight aspects that make the most sense for that audience.

So, the question is: what do you want to tell? What are the relevant aspects of your journey that deserve to be shown and that would help people to know more about you?

The initial impulse of most people is to only share the good things, which there is no problem with. After all, we want to show the world our best version - and we use our Bio to introduce ourselves, adding credibility to our Personal Brand.

Therefore, the first reflection of your Bio can - and should - be about the high points of your career: education, achievements, positions held, projects completed, challenges overcome.

However, not everything good that we have was built in our best moments. So, when writing your Bio, also reflect on: what are the stumbles, mistakes, and lessons learned that you believe are worth sharing?

• Writing Your Bio

There is no right or wrong way to do the Bio. The most important thing is that it is human, written from one person (you) to another (your audiences).

The language should be the one you normally use, as it is also a way to create a connection with your audiences. More than just a "summary" of your story, a good Bio is the authentic and convincing voice of your Brand when you are not present. It can even exude your personality. For this, it is worth dedicating some space to the values, passions, and interests that guide your work, your life, and your world. When your Bio clearly has your voice, you build, in addition to connection, trust and relevance. And you stand out.

It takes courage to infuse personality, passion, and authenticity into what is considered by most people as an "almost resume." We encourage you to step out of your comfort zone and write your biography with the tone of YOUR personality - and with your heart. This way, you will be able to attract the people and opportunities that are right for you.

Below is a guide that can help you develop your Biography.

1. **Have your goal as your guide.** The starting point is not to lose sight of your goal, the one you defined at the beginning of this Personal Brand process. It should be like a guide. Therefore, it is not necessary to write all the passages of your life, but rather the main snapshots of your story, those that are significant to you and to the attributes you want to reinforce at this moment in your life.

2. **Evaluate your current Bio.** If you already have one ready. And mark the sections you want to keep.

3. **Revisit your Unique Value Proposition.** It is your guide. Identify in it and in other content you worked on in Identity, Brand DNA, and Positioning, what are the elements that are authentic, that differentiate you from your peers, and that are convincing to those who will make decisions about you.

4. **Develop a base text, with no character limit.** Make a list of what may be relevant at this moment considering your future goal. Then, turn this list into a text.

Also include:

5. **Values and Passions.** What drives you and what is important to you.

6. **Relevant achievements.** What you do, what you have done that is interesting to your audiences, with your goal in mind.

7. **Engaging facts about you.** Passages or themes that are attractive, fascinating, intriguing even.

8. **Unique characteristics.** What aspects make you "you"?

9. **Credentials.** External validations, awards, testimonials, etc.

10. **Strengths and Differentiators.** What do you do better than anyone else?

11. **Extras.** Add other items that are not on the list above, but that you believe are critical and relevant to express your Personal Brand to the audience you have identified.

Next, see some examples.

Cecília Cavazani, Co-CEO - Cavazani Construtora

Bio: I serve as a co-CEO and partner in a company in the construction industry, specializing in affordable housing. I believe that home ownership is a gateway to many other accomplishments.

I am passionate about my work, and my purpose is to lead the company towards continuous and sustainable growth, enhancing and making exponential our processes and culture, generating value for all involved parties.

Since the beginning of Cavazani Construction's activities, I have been dedicated to delivering results with humanity, fostering a team appreciation culture, and thus, providing affordable housing combined with the experience of owning a first property. My effort is focused on ensuring that the dream of homeownership opens new horizons for our clients and awareness of the value delivered by everyone involved in the projects. I believe that by breaking down barriers of non-belonging, our society will strengthen. I am a lawyer by trade, a marketer by passion, an eternal student, an ambassador of Conscious Capitalism. A friend of words since childhood, I am a poet, a literature lover, a book writer, and a volunteer teacher.

MiniBio: Co-CEO and partner of a company specializing in affordable housing, believes in delivering results with humanity, leads her team towards continuous and sustainable growth, preserving the culture and appreciation of individuals. Lawyer by training, marketer by passion, she is a writer and poet.

Next, the Bio of four female executives, with completely different approaches.

Maitê Leite, Executive Vice President – Institutional, Santander Bank

Maitê Leite is Brazilian, with a degree in Finance from Fundação Armando Álvares Penteado and from the Kellogg School of Management at Northwestern University.

With over 30 years of experience in the financial market across multiple geographies, Maitê joined Santander Brasil in October 2021 as COO Corporate. She is now Executive Vice President – Institutional at Santander Brasil, responsible for Communication, Experience & Culture, the Economic Department, Government Relations, and Sustainability, including initiatives in the Amazon.

She was formerly the CEO and Head of Corporate at Deutsche Bank Brazil. Previously, she served as COO for Latin America and Brazil and was Head of Global Transaction Banking Change Management at Deutsche Bank London. Before that, she held various leadership roles in risk management at Citibank and ABN Amro Brasil. In London, she served as Global COO for Emerging Markets Trading at ABN Amro and RBS Plc.

Passionate about art, nature, and travel, Maitê spends her free time with her family and her three dogs.

Mariana Lorenzon, Supply Chain Director - Mosaic Brazil

Since I was a child, I have felt a desire to transform the environments I entered—fixing what didn't work, organizing the disorganized, making beautiful what was ugly, and lightening what felt heavy. Perhaps the natural path would have been to pursue architecture, but instead, I chose to work in Business Administration, focusing on transforming companies.

Passionate about learning and challenges, I have gained solid experience in Finance, Supply Chain, Marketing, and Sales Operations, holding local, regional, and global roles across different countries (Brazil, France, Germany, and the USA).

Over the last 15 years, I have led multidisciplinary teams, contributing to the transformation of one of the leading innovative companies in the agricultural sector by consistently delivering results through people.

I drive businesses and individuals by demonstrating the impact of authentic, inclusive, and human leadership. Through impactful experiences and real case studies, I can implement deep transformation processes at both corporate and personal levels.

I am an executive with 25 years of experience in a top global agricultural company, with international experience across various functions such as Finance, Supply Chain, and Marketing & Sales. I have a proven track record of developing vision, designing strategies, and executing them in complex and constantly evolving business environments.

I believe in fostering a collaborative, transparent, and inclusive workplace to achieve the best solutions and results. I am not afraid to innovate and take risks—only by doing so do we learn.

Eleonora Lobo Salles Leite, Legal Director - Compliance - ESG, Jervois Brazil

I am a corporate lawyer specializing in mining and metallurgy. I like to say that I just change the metal I work with. I've had the privilege of working with mining projects in the Amazon, in both Pará and Amazonas, engaging closely with traditional and Indigenous communities, participating in impact assessments, and implementing measures to mitigate and compensate those impacts.

Mining may not seem like the friendliest subject, but it is vital for modern life and the continuation of our way of living, driven by technology and innovation.

Currently, I work for a young Australian company entering Brazil with great enthusiasm and a strong desire to make a difference, focusing on becoming a reliable supplier of nickel and cobalt, operating with respect for the highest standards of environmental, social, and safety responsibilities, and ensuring the well-being of our employees and communities.

I love being in an environment where I know I can make a difference—raising awareness among people and the company about the importance of engaging with stakeholders, working hard to minimize negative impacts and create more benefits for surrounding communities.

I am a cheerful and very communicative person, passionate about people and always eager to learn their stories.

Karina Lima, Head of Sales for Startups - Amazon Web Services

From now on, it will always be "Day One."

I am an executive with 20 years of experience in technology sales, a mother to Bento, a wonderful 10-year-old boy, and a proud Carioca.

I am a CIS woman (she/her/ela) and was born and raised in the suburbs of Rio de Janeiro.

In addition to my experience in sales, leadership, and volunteering, I am known for my creative and uncomplicated approach to life, work, and relationships, always putting people first—whether friends, family, employees, or clients.

In my free time, I enjoy the arts, playing the harp, and savoring a good glass of wine.

My career has been driven by a mantra of high performance with purpose, and my core values are empathy, gratitude, and respect. These principles have allowed me to drive business growth across all segments by building diverse, high-performing teams and fostering an environment where people can bring their best while speaking the language of our clients to align our success with theirs.

Half of my professional life has been dedicated to the Startup and Fintech ecosystem, where I am proud to have been involved in companies that began as startups and today positively impact our society.

I am passionate about mentoring and empowering others, especially women, to succeed in their careers and achieve their full potential.

I was the first female Vice President in the core business of my previous employer in Brazil, and through my leadership and advocacy, I helped create a more inclusive and diverse workplace that values and celebrates different perspectives and experiences.

My mother instilled in me the importance of education as the only legacy she could leave me. I earned degrees in Arts and Business, and I continue to prioritize education and self-improvement.

I completed my MBA at Coppead UFRJ and an Advanced Board program at Saint Paul. I also had the opportunity to study Innovation at Kaospilot in Denmark, Behavioral Economics at the University of Chicago, and Governance at Tel Aviv University. Recently, I finished an ESG program at EADA Business School in Barcelona.

I strongly believe in a lifelong learning culture and continuous improvement, striving to apply these principles to both my personal and professional life. With my diverse educational background and extensive experience in technology sales, I look forward to new opportunities and the next exciting chapter with my new team.

Personal Pitch

The elevator pitch, also known as the elevator speech, was created in the 1980s and is a very common practice in Silicon Valley among entrepreneurs. The purpose of this speech is to present an idea in the format of a short and convincing speech to potential investors in a very short amount of time. It originated from the idea that if you were in an elevator with the most important person in the world to buy your idea, whether an investor or the CEO of your company, you cannot miss the opportunity. In this situation, you only have a few seconds, the time it takes to ride the elevator, to present your idea, captivate and make that person interested in learning more and scheduling a meeting with you.

A good personal pitch should be clear, concise, and straight to the point, highlighting the main elements of your Personal Brand, or your business. Basically, it explains what problem you solve and how, emphasizing the main differentiator. It is widely used in networking situations, interviews, business meetings, and social events when you want to make a good impression and establish connections with people. It is a tool for personal use, and never to be written in an email or message. This is because depending on the person you are speaking to – and their receptiveness – you can make adjustments to connect with them. That's why we always recommend having a pitch for each audience you plan to work with. Use it as a prototype, test and adjust it. Your pitch will change, don't worry. And it needs to change. As you continue to "introduce yourself", it's natural to refine and perfect this speech. We ourselves have created more than 50 versions of ours.

Below we share some very specific questions to help you develop your personal pitch, always inspired by the Unique Value Proposition developed in your Positioning.

- Who I am
- What I do for my audience
- Why you are unique
- The result you deliver to your audience

This is the latest version of the pitch I use to start a conversation that is not for one of the specific audiences I target: "I help executives, entrepreneurs, and healthcare professionals identify their differentiators, organizing their narrative authentically and in line with their goals and the needs of their audience. I apply the exclusive FLY® Method for Personal Branding, developed by me and my business partner, using our over 20 years of experience in communication and corporate branding, making something that seems complex simple. Through the Personal Branding methodology, my clients increase business opportunities and engagement with their stakeholders." – Giuliana Tranquilini

As we have discussed in the empathy map, each customer profile has a specific "pain point." It is necessary to create a pitch for each audience, focusing on how you solve that "pain point." Below are examples of pitches for specific audiences to show that you can adjust the same "base" according to the audience's needs.

• Executive Pitch

Imagine me, Giuliana, at a corporate event and an executive who has heard a bit about my work asks me what I do.

"I am a Personal Brand strategist. With over 20 years of experience in corporate branding, **I have developed an exclusive Personal Branding methodology that helps you tell your story authentically to achieve your goals and increase your value in the market.** Shall we schedule a conversation?"

• Pitch for Entrepreneurs to attract investment

Now imagine me introducing myself to an important entrepreneur from Silicon Valley, who could be a potential client for Betafly. See how I adjust my pitch for them:

"I am a Personal Brand strategist. Having a close view of the startup ecosystem, I understand that investors generally don't just bet on a disruptive idea for a scalable business, they will 'buy the entrepreneur', **in other words, your personal brand as an entrepreneur has value in attracting investments.** With my over 20 years of experience working with major brands, I have developed an exclusive MP method where I help entrepreneurs tell their story in an engaging and appealing language to **attract investors.** If you want to know more, shall we grab a coffee?"

- **Pitch for a doctor to attract patients**

In this example, how would I pitch to a doctor who needs to (re) establish their space in a market where new entrants have emerged?

"I am a Personal Brand strategist. With over 20 years of experience in corporate branding, I have developed an exclusive MP method for healthcare professionals where I help you differentiate yourself, have authentic communication **to increase your value to your patients** and have your patients pay for your value, not your price. **This way, you will attract more patients who value your work.** Shall we schedule a conversation?"

Storytelling

Storytelling means "telling stories." We all have stories worth telling, and notice, our minds never stop creating them. We are constantly building positive or negative narratives based on the experiences we live or dream of living. We also tell them without even being aware of a logical structure: at the dinner table, in a social gathering, in the classroom, when presenting an idea in a meeting, speaking to a group of investors, offering a service or product to our clients in an interview.

- **Why tell stories?**

Storytelling is not a new concept, but it has definitely been widely spread in the business world. Especially in Silicon Valley, we find many experts who emphasize the effectiveness of this form of expression. There are numerous studies around the techniques of this ancient act. The most well-known structure is the Hero's Journey, described by Joseph Campbell in his book *The Hero with a Thousand Faces*.[25] This technique describes the 12 steps to create an irresistible story script, widely used by film writer.

Having the ability to tell stories is important for any professional because it is through storytelling that we create an emotional connection to convey a message in an engaging and memorable way. Psychologist and Harvard and Oxford professor Jerome Bruner, for example, found that a fact is 20 times more likely to be remembered if supported by a good narrative. In a study by Carnegie Mellon University, psychologists and neuroscientists discovered that stories stimulate a part of the brain that helps understand the thoughts and emotions of a person. Moreover, they also activate a part of the brain responsible for decision-making and motivation that can prompt the audience to act according to the message conveyed. The brain produces oxytocin, a hormone responsible for promoting empathy and trust - and this helps create an emotional connection between the storyteller and the audience.[26]

Therefore, there is no denying that storytelling is a powerful tool to develop your personal narrative as well - and this can be a great differentiator.

• What story to tell?

The story worth telling is one that resonates, in some way, with your audience, one which has passages that will echo their pains, desires, and dreams, and piques curiosity for the outcome. In general, this often involves sharing about challenges and overcoming them.

When I, Susana, participated in the StoryTalks Workshop, taught by Bruno Scartozzoni, a storytelling expert, and Paulo Ferreira, a

> ## " A FACT IS 20 TIMES MORE LIKELY TO BE REMEMBERED IF SUPPORTED BY A GOOD NARRATIVE."
>
> Jerome Bruner

public speaking and TED Talks preparation expert, I learned from them a powerful rule about storytelling: "Every talk is a snippet." In other words, we will never have time, resources, and opportunities to tell a complete story. Therefore, focus on an episode, choose an aspect, and delve deep into it, extracting its maximum potential. The most powerful narratives can come from seemingly everyday situations but told from a personal perspective.

Practical exercise

Think of a memorable experience, an event that has contributed to shaping who you are today. Don't worry if it seems small or simple - the best stories often come from everyday situations. Use the questions below to identify relevant points that deserve to be shared.

- What was the context, the surroundings?

- What happened that changed the environment?

- How did you react?

- What challenges did you face?

- What decisions did you need to make?

- What skills did you use?

- What values did this experience represent to you?

- Were there outcomes? Did people benefit – learn something, develop themselves?

- What problem did you solve or opportunity did you create?

- In what way did you become better at something?

- What do you know now that you didn't know before this experience?

- What was your feeling after this event?

These questions help extract the maximum potential from an experience. But don't tell your story in bullet points - only use some of these questions as inspiration and start drafting your text in the way you tell (or would tell) it. Try to blend the objectivity of a professional environment with dashes of emotion. And don't forget: the best language to tell a story is your most authentic one!

How to communicate

Think of a person you believe to be an excellent communicator. When we ask this question in our presentations, names like Barack Obama, Michele Obama, and Oprah Winfrey immediately come up as responses. These people have some common characteristics, and it is likely that the person you thought of also has the elements we will describe below. Good communicators have a special talent for delivering their content. This is related to two essential points:

- HOW you handle your content

- HOW you package your content

HOW You Handle Your Content

To effectively communicate your Personal Brand, you need to have clarity, consistency, and constancy. These are the 3 C's of Communication that will give your message strength and relevance. As important as knowing what to communicate is working on these three points. Let's better understand each one of them:

• Clarity

This element is not in first place by chance. Having clear communication is an essential part of any conversation and the success of a brand. Many people believe they communicate well, but when we seek feedback from their audiences, we notice that the message did not always come across as clearly as the sender imagined. As writer Robert McCloskey says: "I know that you believe you understand what you think I said, but I am not sure you realize that what you heard is not what I meant." If people are not able to understand what you intend to do, they will have a hard time connecting with you.

The first golden tip for any communication to be clear is knowing who your audience is, as each audience requires a more suitable language. Let's say you are a doctor speaking to a group of fellow professionals. You can use a more technical language - actually, that is welcomed. However, if you are explaining the same topic to laypeople, you need to be more didactic and aim for a different level of clarity so that your message comes through without distortion. The responsibility

" I KNOW THAT YOU BELIEVE YOU UNDERSTAND WHAT YOU THINK I SAID, BUT I AM NOT SURE YOU REALIZE THAT WHAT YOU HEARD IS NOT WHAT I MEANT."

Robert McCloskey

for understanding a message lies with the sender. So, besides having a grasp of what you want to communicate, you need to think about the language you will use.

Practical Exercise

When crafting a message, try to synthesize in a sentence the result of what you want to leave as a residue.

Step 1 – Use a simple structure like: "What I want people to know is that…" and finish the sentence using this order: subject + verb + Additional Information.

For example: "What I want John to know is that… the project for the new system will be completed next week, and we have solved all the occurring issues."

Step 2 – List the three most relevant topics about this message in a short sentence for each. Using the previous example, we could detail the message as follows:

- the schedule was delayed due to a technical issue

- we have hired an additional team, which will incur extra costs

- despite the delay, the system will be operational in time to serve the new strategy.

When you structure your message in such a simple way, the chance of your message being emitted more clearly is much higher because you have already mentally organized it. When you compose a text without clarity on where you want to go, the chance of the message becoming confusing for the listeners significantly increases.

• Consistency

Consistency in communication is responsible for building trust because it lets your audiences know what to expect from you, strengthening your connection with them. For your communication to be consistent, it is important to have a common thread. In other words, some contents and concepts of your Personal Brand should always be present. The expectation that the next encounter with you will be consistent with the previous ones is what builds reputation. However, there is a point of attention: having a common thread does not mean always being the same. Being consistent, but not predictable, is a goal to be pursued to have a brand perception that is both dynamic and robust.

When we talk about consistent communication for a Personal Brand, we mean that your communication needs to be coherent. You should continuously present yourself in line with your essence. Even when moving through different environments - the company you work in, the school parents' group, tennis class, your social media - ensure that in any setting, you can reinforce your positioning and the DNA of your brand. Of course, you will adapt the content based on the context, but make sure your key messages are being conveyed.

An example of consistency is how journalist Ana Paula Padrão communicates. Known for a solid career as an international correspondent and presenter, Ana Paula founded a platform supporting female entrepreneurship in 2004. Since then, her communication consistently brings elements of women empowerment, quickly becoming a reference in this area. Another example is presenter Luciano Huck, who, despite having a successful career, built a narrative closely tied to social concerns.

The common thread should always run through your communication so your audience can "grasp" that message and, therefore, always associate your brand with it. For example, in all the workshops, mentorships, and conversations we have about Personal Branding, we like to reinforce that self-knowledge is the pillar supporting any authentic brand. The common thread is self-knowledge, which reinforces our Positioning. This ensures that most people interacting with us know that a Personal Branding journey with Betafly will be a process with greater depth and authenticity.

Eduardo worked for many years in the consumer goods sector. When he reached out to us, it had been five years since he transitioned to a B2B company. He wanted to return to working for a company directly serving the end consumer because he believed that in this business model, he could better utilize his skills. Upon receiving the results of his 360° Feedback, we noticed that his Personal Brand was diffuse: some people still recognized him in the old sector and only had that memory. Others only knew the Eduardo from the current sector and seemed unsure about his most relevant previous experiences.

Having worked in different sectors could be a significant advantage for Eduardo, but it was turning into a real setback. Instead of showcasing himself as a professional with diversified experience, he gave the impression of lacking a distinct performance trait. In organizing the key messages of his brand, we aimed to find a common thread and concluded that his concern for sustainability, governance, and ethics was something that united his various experiences. Therefore, these three points became his main message. From that point on, it became much easier for people to understand the contribution Eduardo could make wherever he was working, regardless of his position. This greatly facilitated his discourse, and he quickly managed to reposition himself in the sector he was seeking.

Practical Exercise

Reflect on the recent communications of your Personal Brand. They can be networking meetings, event participations, posts, speeches, presentations you've given, any opportunity where you introduced yourself or professionally interacted. Evaluate if there is a common thread in them, an element that you repeat about your professional value proposition. Assess if this element is what you would like to be remembered for by others. Keep this reflection as it is a warm-up for you to begin working on enhancing your communication.

• Constancy

To have constancy is to be visible and have frequency in communication. Time is one of the greatest allies in strengthening brands.

Strong brands are always on the radars of their audiences and create trust in their deliveries by always being there. Many people communicate something once or twice and think that's enough. This is a big mistake because few people receive one hundred percent of the impacts we emit. So, do not fear repetition. Saying the same thing multiple times, and from different angles has several advantages. One of them is that not everyone understands right away what you mean. It may seem obvious to you, but what you are saying is not always clear to someone else. Repetition helps with clarity. Another advantage is memorization. By receiving information for a long period, the brain starts to consolidate that message in long-term memory, making it easier to access later. In a world with so much noise and distractions, persisting in exploring the full potential of a message can be of great value for strengthening your Personal Brand.

Practical exercise

If the success of a Personal Branding work relies on consistency, it is very important that you dedicate yourself to it regularly. Do not set tasks that are too impossible to accomplish because it's no use acting with high intensity for a week and then stop because you can't sustain the pace.

You might ask us: How do people manage to produce so much content? I can barely keep up with my schedule. How can I do this? The key is to prioritize, and it requires a change in habits. It's a pattern break, incorporating the habit.

Keeping the frequency can be a challenge for some people, but that doesn't mean you need to become a slave to content production. To solve this issue, evaluate:

How much time in your week do you spend working on the Personal Branding of others?

And how much time do you dedicate to your own?

James Clear, author of the book Atomic Habits, says, "Consistency comes before intensity. Start small and become the type of person who shows up every day. (...) And then increase the intensity."[27]

Set a goal for content production and sharing that makes sense to you, and that you consider possible to achieve, regardless of the medium you choose.

Block a weekly time for it – put it in your schedule as if it were a meeting with someone else. If you have to cancel, immediately reschedule another time. Taking communication consistency seriously is a fundamental step for the success of your Personal Brand. Important: interacting, responding to messages, commenting on social media, and being active with your audience is also being visible.

" CONSISTENCY COMES BEFORE INTENSITY. START SMALL AND BECOME THE TYPE OF PERSON WHO SHOWS UP EVERY DAY. (...) AND THEN INCREASE THE INTENSITY."

James Clear

HOW You Package Your Content

Have you ever wondered why some people have a more memorable presence than others when approaching the same content?

We call Executive Presence the set of subtle elements that involve Personal Branding and that lead some people to have a more memorable presence than others.

We all know extremely competent people with a lot of content and the ability to organize their narratives in a logical way, but who cannot stand out in the environment they are in. The opposite also exists. People who do not have a great differential but, colloquially speaking, "make an entrance". These people seem to have something difficult to explain, which has been called aura, charisma, magnetism, and various other names composed of subjective elements.

Until some time ago, it was believed that this aura was a gift, a natural gift. Either you were lucky to be an individual born blessed with this talent, or, unfortunately, you had to settle for your fate.

Fortunately, this has changed, and today there are several professionals dedicated to studying and dissecting the main elements that make someone have a more impactful presence than others.

I, Susana, had the privilege of being in New York with Harrison Monarth, an executive coach, leadership consultant, and discussing with him the details of his approach in the excellent and best-selling book Executive Presence. Presence, in the strict sense, is the opposite of absence, and according to Harrison, it is literally what we are talking about: being there when people need you. "It is a fluid concept that encompasses certain characteristics, behaviors, skills, and personality traits that make up a personal power that inspires and engages people."[28]

We will explore here two aspects of this fascinating theme.

Emotional and Social Intelligence

When the two of us worked at Natura, we learned a concept that enchanted us, whose essence still accompanies us today: well-being and being well. This phrase is formed from a continuous connection between well-being (internal, being well with oneself) and being well (external, being well with the world) and expresses how these two dimensions connect in a flow that manifests in harmonious relationships.

Harrison Monarth says, "Self-awareness is about understanding oneself and how you behave in contact with other people. Social Intelligence is, therefore, much about how you are perceived by other people, or better yet, managing what is perceived by other people. It is about understanding – and when you understand correctly, mastering - what elicits a positive response from others in terms of relationships and casual encounters as well as in front of an audience full of strangers."

In order to have harmonious relationships, we need a competence to manage feelings. In 1995, psychologist Daniel Goleman coined this ability emotional intelligence when he released the bestseller *Emotional Intelligence*, with millions of copies sold worldwide. According to his approach, emotional intelligence is formed by five fundamental principles: self-awareness, emotional control, self-motivation, empathy, and social skills (social intelligence).

The five pillars developed by Goleman are:

1. **Self-awareness:** knowing your emotions and understanding how they work. How they arise, where they come from, and how they manifest. People who know themselves are aware of their strengths, weaknesses, and limitations, learn to explore their potential and respect their limits.

2. **Self-regulation:** the ability to control your emotions, manage your feelings. After recognizing what you feel, it becomes easier to control these different sensations. The ability to deal with adverse situations, maintaining control and security, in a positive and less stressful way.

3. **Self-motivation:** using emotions to your advantage, in favor of some objective, motivating yourself and staying motivated. Perseverance, resilience, and initiative are characteristics of self-motivated people.

4. **Empathy:** This pillar already involves interpersonal skills, not just individual skills. Recognizing that other people around you also have their emotions and need to learn to deal with them. Recognizing emotions in others. Feeling the other in a social environment, perceiving their pains and needs, having empathy.

> **" IT IS A FLUID CONCEPT THAT ENCOMPASSES CERTAIN CHARACTERISTICS, BEHAVIORS, SKILLS, AND PERSONALITY TRAITS THAT MAKE UP A PERSONAL POWER THAT INSPIRES AND ENGAGES PEOPLE."**
>
> Harrison Monarth

5. **Interpersonal Relationship:** the need to relate to others and how social skills can be useful in this sense. Interacting in a social environment. Being emotionally available, persuasive, influential, and knowing how to manage conflicts.

By working on these aspects, your communication gains power by being anchored in who you are when in balance. Bringing it to Personal Branding, we see that being in balance with oneself and with the environment is essential to launching oneself into the world. Therefore, it is important to first look inward, exercising self-awareness, and then look outward and understand how this "self" will position itself in the chess game called the market.

Nonverbal Communication

Nonverbal communication is the transmission of information, feelings, and intentions without the use of words. In other words, everything that also communicates, such as gestures, eye contact, facial expressions, body posture, tone and speed of voice, and other aspects that do not involve spoken or written language, and that complement the meaning of words. The way we present ourselves to the world directly influences how we are perceived by others. By conveying coherent, authentic, and positive communication through nonverbal communication, we are reinforcing our Personal Brand and strengthening a consistent and memorable image.

These elements, together with the meaning of words, make up the whole message we are emitting. One of the leading scholars in this subject was the Iranian professor Albert Mehrabian, who conducted extensive research at UCLA (University of California, Los Angeles) and published a book that became a reference on this subject, Silent Messages. Mehrabian found that nonverbal language greatly impacts the perception of the feelings behind the message being conveyed while composing the whole. For example, a confident and upright posture can convey authority and security, while a hunched posture may give off an image of submission or insecurity. A genuine smile can convey empathy and sympathy, while a closed expression can be interpreted as hostility or disinterest.

Professor Mehrabian's reasoning is that words, voice, and body language should be consistent with each other during communication. If the information interpreter detects any inconsistency, it will be the nonverbal aspect that is primarily used to form an overall impression of the message.

Practical exercise

Want to know how your nonverbal communication is like? Choose a comfortable topic for you – for example, a part of your life that you often talk about, so you don't have to worry about memorizing the content. Record yourself speaking and then watch it while observing the following aspects:

- Eye contact
- Body posture
- Body and arm movements
- Head direction
- Modulation of your voice
- Silence and use of pauses.

When watching your video, more than focusing on technical aspects, evaluate if your nonverbal communication conveys the feelings you want to express and if they contribute to helping understand your message.

Some considerations on how to evaluate your nonverbal communication while watching your video, and how you can ensure to convey what you desire naturally.

Voice Tone

Every brand has a "voice" that is an expression of its personality. For example, your voice can be friendly, passionate, polite, witty, familiar, direct , or reserved.

It is important to avoid a frequent confusion here: when we talk about the voice of the Personal Brand, we are talking about the attributes of your communication, that is, what your voice conveys, what people feel when they hear, read, or see something produced by you.

Yes, the "voice" of your brand is how you express yourself.

The voice of your Brand is a characteristic of your personality, and most of the time, it is what predominates in your communication because it is already part of you, it is what you do effortlessly. But you can "calibrate" the tone of your voice according to the intention of your communication. Your tone is how you express your personality in a specific situation. Depending on your audience and the intention of your communication, the emotional state of the audience, and other relevant contextual factors, you may want to adapt the tone of your voice.

Note that we are not talking about the timbre of your voice! And what is the difference between timbre and tone?

Timbre is the more technical characteristic of your voice: a voice can be deep, nasal, high-pitched... In fact, there are studies, like one conducted by Duke University in the United States, that indicate that a deeper voice leads to greater success in one's career.

The tone is what you convey through your voice: optimism, confidence... An example: most of the time, your communication may be more enthusiastic and energetic. This does not prevent you from using an optimistic and persuasive tone in a sales communication, a cautious and humble tone in an apology email to your patients or clients. This is adjusting the tone of your voice according to your audience and goals.

When you bring the tone of your voice to the level of awareness and use it more intentionally, your brand becomes more aligned with what you want to project. Indeed, becoming aware of any aspect of nonverbal communication helps use it more strategically.

Physical Presentation

It is an element that people often directly associate with Executive Presence. It's no wonder. The way we present ourselves is the first impression we make, even before we have had the opportunity to present our content.

We have all heard that the brain takes very few seconds to form a first impression. And we know how first impressions are biased by cultural elements. For example, in the West, a man wearing a stylish, well-tailored suit may be considered a good professional, even before his competence is known. Similarly, a woman with her hair in a perfect bun, well-done makeup, and an impressive accessory can communicate seniority. In India or the East, the attire to communicate these same attributes may be completely different. Codes vary according to culture. Millions of people worldwide saw Tamim bin Hamad Al Thani, monarch and head of state of Qatar, drape a gold-thread embroidered tunic over the shoulders of player Lionel Messi at the presentation of the 2022 World Cup trophy. Few understood the significance since it is an attire that means nothing outside of that context. In that country, however, it symbolizes royalty and is only worn on very special occasions.

Codes, which vary according to the environment you are interacting in, will send messages about you implicitly. That is why there are many professionals dedicated to supporting people in presenting themselves in a way that aligns with the image they want to portray - from style consultants to speech therapists.

We recognize that these elements are powerful, but we believe that more important than trying to conform to a standard is presenting oneself in alignment with one's Identity. Like almost everything in life, wisdom is usually found in the middle. We recommend that you strive to have an authentic image while also incorporating elements that are comfortable for your audience. This is often a good recipe. This way, you can maintain a personal style over time.

Avoid at all costs trying to build an image based soley on a character. This requires a great deal of energy, almost as if attacking who you truly are. And it is very difficult to sustain. A classic and widely discussed case in Silicon Valley (and beyond) was that of entrepreneur Elizabeth Holmes, who is currently imprisoned and serving time for fraud. Holmes deceived various investors with a project that did not actually exist, but the point we want to address here is that she tried to create a persona that she believed would communicate elements of success as an entrepreneur. The two most striking symbols she adopted were: first, wearing black turtleneck tops identical to the ones Steve Jobs wore in almost all of his public presentations. And the second was working on her voice to sound slightly deeper than it naturally was. There is a recording that shows Holmes "slipping" and using her natural voice tone, then quickly reverting to a deeper tone. Holmes is one of the numerous examples of people who try to construct a character but are unable to sustain it for long. Authenticity and genuine communication, when supporting content that is relevant to others, are powerful elements of impactful presence.

Where to Communicate

Some of the channels for expressing your Personal Brand are meetings, events, presentations, coffee meet ups. In addition to these, there is the online environment with social media, email marketing, websites. There are many opportunities to showcase your attributes, but you don't need to be everywhere. Let's talk about these different options and help you choose which ones to prioritize based on the goals of your Personal Branding.

Online Communication

Online communication amplifies the possibility of connecting with your audiences. It has a greater or lesser weight depending on various factors, such as your field of work, the position you hold, and the nature of your work. Today, however, there are very few roles in which we identify that digital channels do not have a positive collaboration.

We know that some people are still very resistant to these channels and prefer face-to-face communication. One thing does not replace the other. The objectives of each channel and form of communication are different. Mastering the calibration of these two elements and deciding when it is best to use one or the other is powerful in favor of building your Personal Brand.

Social media are one of the main tools for strengthening your Personal Brand, and generally, they are the gateway to new clients. These are places where you will be constantly communicating through content determined by your key messages. You can use Youtube, podcasts, apps, WhatsApp, Instagram, Facebook, Telegram, LinkedIn, and newsletters.

Presence on social media should be a dialogue, an exchange, and interaction with your community. This brings the possibility of getting to know your audiences even more and obtaining feedback that can guide actions in your business and content on social media. In addition to listening to what people say about you, it is important to interact with your community to redirect your communication and your business, reinforcing your brand attributes for which you want to be recognized.

Through this dialogue, you build trust, make the relationship more mature, and whenever your community needs your services, they will remember or even recommend you.

Therefore, this is a great opportunity to "mark" your territory and your Positioning!

A very common question we receive is: "Do I need to be on all social media?" The answer is no. There is no need to be present on all of them, nor to develop content for all available channels. You have to choose the most relevant social network for your business, aligned and consistent with your essence, and most importantly, where your audience is. Only if you have time available to manage more than one digital network, or a team to do so, should you work on the second one. The most important thing is to have one done well.

The questions that help in this process are:

- Where is the audience I want to reach?

- What is my affinity with the network?

- What resources do I have (schedule, people) to feed this network?

It is important to know each social network or online communication channel to define which and how to use it, besides understanding what your audience expects from each one. Below, we have listed the main idea of each platform so that you can delve deeper when choosing which ones to use to strengthen your brand and maintain a connection with your audience:

- **LinkedIn:** A network with a more professional profile, which has been growing more and more as a digital channel to build authority. You can be part of discussion groups according to your professional interest, share articles, posts, and videos. It is the essential network for executives and entrepreneurs to use as a powerful networking tool, being able to connect with other professionals from anywhere in the world.

- **Instagram:** It is a network where users like to follow quick information supported by visual resources. The audience is primarily female, and in Brazil, it has been widely used for fashion, beauty, health, and wellness businesses. It is also possible to boost posts and target audiences by interests, age, and geographic location. In the United States, Instagram is not the primary network for contacts and generating business. Through this platform, you can create targeted ads to reach your most interested audience.

- **Facebook:** A platform with a profile more geared towards lead generation in specific audiences. It is also possible to create targeted ads to reach your audience. It is important to evaluate if your audience frequently uses this platform.

- **Twitter:** A social network focused on microblogs, with short and direct messages. It is mainly used to share ideas, opinions, and stay updated on news and trends.

- **YouTube:** Efficient for high-quality and long-lasting content, videos can be searched for years after their creation in a more organized way, in lists (instead of the feed). Usually, it is a more active online platform for Personal Brands and is often used as a secondary option along with Instagram, LinkedIn, or Facebook.

- **TikTok:** Focused on short and viral videos, quick, creative, fun, dynamic content. If you have a young audience, consider it. According to the platform's data, 66% of users are under 30 years old, with the majority between 16 and 24 years old.

- **WhatsApp:** For quick conversations, it has been used very frequently for contacting individual clients or groups of friends and discussions.

- **Telegram:** It has been used for groups, where it is possible to share more exclusive content and participants do not have access to all "open" contacts as in WhatsApp.

Practical Exercise: Define your goals for online communication

Strengthen your objectives. What is success for you with your online communication?

- Increasing visibility for your Personal Brand and also for your business?

- Increasing interaction with your audiences?

- Reinforcing your credibility in your field of work?

- All of the above?

Based on your definition of success, think about goals for your communication that will help you achieve your objectives. Set them according to your routine, what fits into your daily life, and what you will be able to achieve. Remember that generating content is something that takes time. Therefore, we recommend organizing your schedule to carry out this task and meet your goal of being present on social media consistently.

In-person Communication for Audiences

Speaking to large audiences, in lectures, talks, TV programs... can be daunting for some people - studies show that over 80% of the population suffers from strong anxiety when speaking in public - preparing for these situations is important because it is another opportunity to amplify your message. Face-to-face communication is almost unbeatable for some situations. It is when we can use elements such as empathy, reading the other person's needs, sensitivity, among many other skills... With eye contact, we can adapt our communication and message for a better fit in each situation.

This great opportunity to strengthen our Personal Brand can create the famous butterflies in the stomach before stepping onto the stage. This anxiety is natural and explained by science as almost a survival instinct. Therefore, our goal here is not to overcome anxiety, but to manage it. To put this powerful feeling to work in your favor. Being comfortable speaking in public is important not only for you to feel better but also to increase the audience's interest in your message. Watching an anxious person also makes the audience uncomfortable, and therefore, decreases their level of engagement. Professor Matt Abrahams presents three tips that can help manage this feeling.

1. **Usually, anxiety appears at the beginning or before the presentation. Instead of trying to control this feeling, acknowledge it.** Tell yourself something like: "yes, I am feeling this way because this is an important moment for me and the results have consequences for my professional image." Simply recognizing the feeling does not reduce it, but it prevents it from escalating to much higher levels.

2. **Do not see a presentation as a performance.** In a performance, such as theater or dance, there is a right and wrong. In a presentation, there is not. See it as a conversation. To do this, start by asking questions, using colloquial language and inclusive language.

3. **Focus on the present moment instead of worrying about future consequences.** Some techniques that can help include doing a quick meditation beforehand, as well as using breathing and vocal warm-up techniques.

Another resource that helps you prepare for a presentation is to have a clear picture in your mind of what people need to retain as the main message after your speech. It could be a gain, a lesson learned, or a feeling provoked. Ask yourself: "What do people need to have understood by the end of my presentation?" "What is the main feeling you want to evoke in these people?" Another tip: do not leave this message for the end, put it at the beginning of your speech and continue explaining. This way, your narrative will be much more fluid and efficient.

Your presentation can be supported and differentiated by slides, but be careful not to use them as a crutch. The intention is for them to complement your message, illustrating something with an image that is difficult to convey in words and even guiding your presentation. Do not have slides with a lot of text, and, especially, avoid reading what is written on them. The more comfortable you become in a presentation, the less you will need them.

A challenge in the smartphone era is to retain the audience's attention. Instead of fighting the fact that people keep their phones on while you speak, propose an activity that involves the device to engage the audience. Some suggestions:

- Questions and answers on apps that display results on the screen;

- Suggest questions to be sent to people who are not at the event, asking for a short and quick response that can help connect with concepts you are discussing;

- Interaction and real-time posting on the event's own social network.

Finally, although it may be tempting to rehearse your script until late at night, do not do it. What you need to have memorized has already been internalized. Your body and mind will be much better prepared for the performance if you get a good night's sleep and eat well.

Networking

The word networking gives many people chills. If this is your case, before skipping this content, please give us credit: we will try to change your mind. This concept, old and poorly done, does not yield results and only harms the perception that people have of you. It is like the confusion made between Personal Branding vs. self-promotion.

If you already believe in the importance of cultivating professional relationships, let's delve into this topic so relevant to your career. Networking is not about accepting invitations to boring meetings and then subjecting yourself to inconvenient follow-ups from people interested in selling something or asking for favors. That is dealing with self-interested individuals. Networking is not a selfish act, something like: "How can this person benefit me?" If it is built with a purely commercial intention, it can even harm your reputation. In the book *Taking the Work Out of Networking – An Introvert's guide to Making Connections That Count*, author Karen Wickre, a communicator and connector of people, conducted a survey to find out what bothered people the most when they realized they were the target of a self-interested networking attempt. The majority responded that when making this type of connection, one has to force a persona. This, most of the time, instead of connecting, ends up "disconnecting."

True and positive networking is about building genuine selfless relationships – yet interesting – over time. It is a genuine belief in the power of human relationships and all the positive things they can bring to our lives.

Social psychologist and Stanford organizational behavior professor Brian Lowery presents a provocative and powerful theory of Identity in his book *Selfless: The Social Creation of 'You'*, arguing that we are products of our relationships, social creations of those with whom we interact. Therefore, we are not islands, but the result of the many hands that touch us. We do not exist only in communities but are created and shaped by them. Our highs and lows are not just ours but also belong to others. Business and opportunities are consequences of these relationships, happening naturally over time.

In his book *Give and Take*, Adam Grant explains the nature of these relationships. According to Grant, people fall into the categories of givers, matchers, and takers in how they approach their relationships, and surprisingly, givers are the ones who, over time, achieve more success in their careers.

When I, Susana, participated in a program on Executive Presence, Influence, and Persuasive Leadership at the Wharton School, I had the opportunity to learn from Professor Cade Massey about social capital. I really liked this concept, which is a way of saying that each of us, as professionals, accumulates a "relational capital" throughout our careers, and that this is indeed an asset that can differentiate us from other professionals. Well-connected individuals in their field, whether within the organizations they are part of or the groups they participate in, associations, generally understand the major movements within their niche and know what lies behind the decisions that have been made. In other words, they can see the strategic landscape in a broader way because they are immersed in that context and

" **THEREFORE, WE ARE NOT ISLANDS, BUT THE RESULT OF THE MANY HANDS THAT TOUCH US. WE DO NOT EXIST ONLY IN COMMUNITIES BUT ARE CREATED AND SHAPED BY THEM."**

Brian Lowery

have many connections within it. For example, doctors in a specific specialty know each other and meet in clinic corridors, hospitals, or at conferences. Marketing professionals know each other within companies, accumulate former colleagues, and build relationships in their field naturally. These networks formed by individuals who operate in the same context are called "dense" networking networks. In general, it does not require much effort to be in this type of network, since the people in it are part of your daily life and speak the same language.

In addition to dense networks, there is another type called "dispersed" networking networks. These are the ones you form by interacting outside your usual sphere of activity.

For example: you are a marketing professional but seek to talk with those in logistics, have relationships with HR... You may take a class in gastronomy, music, or arts and thus further expand your network of contacts, engaging with people with diverse backgrounds from yours who are interested in different subjects. Coming from different contexts, they bring new information and perspectives... Therefore, the advantage of having a dispersed network is both the increase in connections and content. A study conducted by Ronald S. Burt, a professor of sociology and strategy at the University of Chicago Booth School of Business, showed that these individuals, by receiving inputs from diverse environments, achieve greater professional mobility and are more capable of bringing innovation to their work.

According to him: "An idea that is mundane in one group can be a valuable insight in another." The professor demonstrates that by building diversified networks, we become bridges (or intermediaries) between different social or professional groups, which gives us more possibilities of having a good idea.

An important point that Professor Massey mentioned in his class is that many of us want to reap the benefits of a vibrant and active network but do not step out of our comfort zone. If we do not seek diversity in contacts today, in the present, it will not be possible to reap the benefits of a "dispersed" network in the future. Our suggestion, therefore, is to start expanding your relationships today.

Having a powerful networking network requires time, energy, and dedication to produce significant results. This is a long process. So, the sooner you start, the more fruits you will reap. Being strategic when it comes to networking is not about making connections only when you need to change jobs or need something. Aim to create a network and the habit of building relationships without expecting anything in return. This may include sharing useful information, providing constructive feedback, offering help or resources to the person, or even being available to listen and support others' needs.

Genuine and selfless relationships over time, but seeking out interesting contacts and conversations, are what usually bear fruit - when least expected! Trust in the law of reciprocity, and at some point, you will be "rewarded." It may be that the person with whom you had a relationship recommends you for a project or praises your work and value in a way that is crucial for closing a deal.

I, Giuliana, when I moved to Palo Alto and experienced firsthand what it's like to build a network from scratch - and how important it is to make a habit of connecting with people. Living here has taught me much more about networking, because I am in an environment of innovation, where the practice of diversity of people and ideas happens daily. So, people are open to understanding others. When I send a message on LinkedIn to someone I don't know, suggesting a "virtual coffee", without selling or offering anything, just asking for some of their time to hear about their expertise, for example, I rarely go without a response. In 99% of the messages, I can schedule a virtual conversation. After that first contact, I try to keep myself "visible", at least on the social networks of these people.

AN IDEA THAT IS MUNDANE IN ONE GROUP CAN BE A VALUABLE INSIGHT IN ANOTHER."

Ron S. Burt

Building and maintaining genuine long-term relationships is a skill and a daily task that should be taught in the classroom. Networking is about relationships and relationships are about trust. So, build trust first and develop your relationships. We, as social beings, value this. Cultivate your relationships and learn to care. Leave a positive impression. Networking is a continuous process that should be treated with care and has a lot to add to your Personal Brand.

Giuliana entered my life as a pleasant surprise at a moment when I was completing a decade of work in my practice. Medical marketing books always warn that this ten-year mark is often a peak, a plateau where growth becomes minimal, more akin to arithmetic progression than geometric. I felt an urge to understand what I had built up to that point.

I remember hearing a phrase recently that struck me: "You can't read the label from inside the bottle." That was exactly the perspective I needed. I needed to empower myself by understanding who I was and what I had achieved—and that is no easy task.

At that moment, I reached out to Haruê, a childhood friend and schoolmate, who told me about Giuliana. She mentioned someone she trusted who offered mentorship in branding, and I found the idea fascinating—especially because it was a recommendation from a friend and coach. I got in touch, and we had our first meeting. We set our goals and began the mentoring process.

I eagerly looked forward to those weekly sessions because the conversations were enriching and always mutually beneficial. I was open to new things, and the learning and discussions were incredibly engaging. It was like having a psychologist by my side.

In the end, I can say the work we did together was truly beautiful. Many friends who went through the same phase I was in, seeking to rediscover themselves and struggling with the "underdog syndrome," found in Giuliana a valuable recommendation. I always recommend her for her professionalism, dedication, and excellence in the services she provides.

From this mentorship, I carry a lifelong appreciation—Giuliana became someone special in my life, and I am deeply grateful for her commitment and efforts beyond expectations. In a world where it is rare to find professionals who truly deliver on their promises, Giuliana stands out.

Dr. Jefferson Medeiros,
Head and Neck Surgeon - Founder of Clínica Dr. Jefferson Medeiros -
Host of Jeff Podcast, Founder of O Ponto Final for doctors, and CBN Columnist

CHAPTER 10

ARTIFICIAL INTELLIGENCE
AND THE FUTURE
OF PERSONAL BRANDING

When this book was written between 2022 and 2023, generative artificial intelligence was just beginning to make waves with the release of ChatGPT. Now, in 2024, the landscape has become even more dynamic and rapidly evolving, demanding that professionals and brands adapt quickly. We are living in an era of accelerated transformations. Since the explosion of generative AI in 2023, the world has undergone profound changes, directly impacting the way Personal Brands are managed. Today, people have access to technologies that amplify their voices, expand their presence, and enable the creation of personalized content at an unprecedented speed and consistency.

In this context of technological advancements, one of the greatest challenges for professionals and brands is to find the balance between leveraging automated tools and preserving authenticity. With AI expanding exponentially across all areas of communication—from customer service to content creation—a legitimate concern arises: is the use of these technologies distancing people from the human essence in their interactions?

This concern stems from the fear that over-reliance on technology might erode the ability to express oneself genuinely. After all, in a world where algorithms mediate so many experiences, the fear that the "human touch" might be lost is both real and pervasive. However, what many fail to fully grasp is that authenticity cannot be automated. The true power of AI lies in its ability to streamline processes, automate repetitive tasks, and free up space for individuals to focus on what truly matters: being more in tune with their own essence.

Authenticity, the cornerstone of a strong Personal Brand, cannot be replaced by technology. AI should not be seen as a threat to our humanity but rather as a powerful tool that helps us become more authentic by freeing up time and energy for what really counts: developing genuine human connections and telling authentic stories.

" NO MATTER HOW MUCH TECHNOLOGY ADVANCES, NOTHING CAN REPLACE THE POWER OF STORIES."

Russ Altman

The Automation Paradox: Streamlining to Connect

Rather than distancing us, AI can bring us closer to people if used wisely. Automated tools, such as those used for behavior analysis or content planning, may not have the power to generate empathy, tell stories, or create emotional connections—but they can provide us with more time to focus on these critical activities. A clear example is the automation of repetitive tasks, like scheduling social media posts, which allows content creators to dedicate more attention to creativity and the development of authentic messaging.

AI helps us organize, structure, and amplify our communications, but the heart of the message must remain human. It can suggest the optimal times to post or identify engagement patterns, but it will never replace the impact of a real story, told with emotion and empathy.

The Personal Brand of the Future: Balancing Technology and Humanity

The personal brand of the future will be defined by a careful balance between the use of innovative technologies and the preservation of human authenticity. Russ Altman, a professor of Bioengineering, Genetics, Medicine, and Biomedical Data Science at Stanford, highlighted a key point on the *Think Fast, Talk Smart* podcast with Matt Abrahams: "If you're worried that an AI tool could replace you, it's time to reflect on how clear your communication really is." He suggests that instead of threatening authenticity, AI pushes us to be even clearer and more deliberate in what we want to say. Therefore, the challenge is not to compete with AI but to use it to amplify what makes us distinctly human.

To achieve this, it is essential to have a deep understanding of who we are and what we represent. Authentic content, whether in written form, video, or public speaking, cannot be generated by an algorithm—it must emerge from our stories, experiences, and our ability to create meaningful connections.

Being intentional in the use of technology is critical. AI can organize data, suggest strategies, and even draft outlines for text, but the final touch—the one that truly creates impact—must come from a human. The strongest personal brands of the future will be those that skillfully integrate these tools without losing sight of their core humanity. These will be the brands that manage to maintain empathy and humanity at the center of everything they do.

Human Narratives in an Automated World

No matter how much technology advances, nothing can replace the power of stories. As Altman emphasizes, it's the stories people remember that create connections. AI may help with data analysis and structuring information, but the true impact of a Personal Brand will always come from the story it tells. And that story must reflect genuine emotions, experiences, and values.

The key takeaway here is that AI, by freeing up our time for more creative and deeper work, offers us the opportunity to refine our narratives. It encourages us to think more profoundly about who we are and what we want to communicate to the world. The more automated the world becomes, the more crucial it will be for the stories we tell to be authentic, unique, and unmistakably ours.

How to Build an Authentic Personal Brand in the Age of AI

Here are a few guidelines to ensure your Personal Brand remains authentic, even in an increasingly automated world:

1. **Use AI as a support, not a substitute:** Automation can increase efficiency, but the heart of your message must be genuine and come from you.

2. **Humanize your digital interactions:** Whenever possible, add a personal touch. This could be through video messages, audio notes, or small gestures of empathy.

3. **Tell your story:** AI can help structure your content, but the narrative must reflect your personal experiences, values, and vision.

4. **Be intentional:** Every AI tool you use should serve a clear purpose. Leverage technology strategically to emphasize your humanity.

5. **Be transparent:** If you're using AI to assist in communication, be open about it. Transparency builds trust.

The Future of Personal Branding: Technology and Humanity, Side by Side

The future of Personal Branding will not be dictated solely by technology or automation, but by the ability to balance the digital with the human. As we surround ourselves with more automated tools, it becomes even more critical that these tools serve our true essence. In a world of algorithms and predictive analytics, authenticity will be the ultimate differentiator.

This chapter, discussing AI, was co-authored with the assistance of generative AI.

" THE FUTURE OF PERSONAL
BRANDING WILL NOT
BE DICTATED SOLELY BY
TECHNOLOGY OR AUTOMATION,
BUT BY THE ABILITY TO
BALANCE THE DIGITAL
WITH THE HUMAN."

CHAPTER 11

PUTTING YOUR
PERSONAL BRAND
INTO ACTION

Y ou have traveled through an intense and profound journey of self-reflection on how you want the world to perceive your Personal Brand. Now we invite you to put into practice the insights you have gained throughout this process – we hope there have been many!

The success of this journey starts with the Communication Strategy that needs to be executed with intention. Intention is the motivating force that will drive your actions. Ideally, from now on, your actions should be permeated by it. At all times, when communicating, relating, presenting yourself, dressing, in every opportunity you have, act with intention and reinforce the attributes that you want to be alive in people's minds. In this way, you will stack the bricks of your Personal Brand so that it grows and gains strength.

Knowing what you know now, do not tire of asking yourself: "What would I do differently from what I have been doing so far to shape a perception of my Personal Brand aligned with my goals?" To support you in this, create an action plan. To answer this question, consolidate your reflections so far - the "Practical Exercises" in a list of actions, and make a commitment to yourself. When we move from thought to writing, we better organize what we wish to do.

The action plan is like a "treasure map," it is the sequence of steps you will take to put your Communication Strategy into practice. While intention seemed abstract, now is the time to make it concrete.

The main driver of a plan is your goal (or set of goals). It is your ultimate objective - what you want to achieve. From there, the actions you will take should be defined. Ayelet Fishbach, a professor of Behavioral

Science and Marketing at the University of Chicago Booth School of Business, and a great scholar of motivation, explains that goals cannot be too abstract, or it becomes difficult to establish the tasks that need to be executed to reach them.[35] For example, if you determine that you want to "be a relevant professional," it will be difficult to establish what tasks you need to do to be relevant, as this is a word that has many possible interpretations. On the other hand, if you decide that, for your professional goals, it is important to expand your networking, it becomes clearer how to develop a task list. For example:

- Research the main events in my industry for the next semester, and register for at least 3;

- Set a contact goal for each of these events;

- Reconnect with people A , B, C;

- Make X new connections on LinkedIn per week...

" GOALS CANNOT BE TOO ABSTRACT, OR IT BECOMES DIFFICULT TO ESTABLISH THE TASKS THAT NEED TO BE EXECUTED TO REACH THEM."

Ayeler Fishback

To distinguish these concepts well, Ayelet recommends asking two types of questions: the "why" type of question helps define your goals, and the "how" type of question helps define the tasks.

A good format for an action plan is the well-known 5W2H: a set of questions used to develop action plans quickly and efficiently. It is quite popular in companies, and although not a new tool, it is current and works well to organize the tasks that need to be executed. It helps ensure that a project is planned clearly and completely, defining each step that needs to be taken. Its combination of letters was borrowed from English, in the following composition:

- **What (what will be done):** describe clearly the activity or task to be performed.

- **Why (why it will be done):** defines the reason or justification for the task.

- **Who (by whom it will be done):** identifies the person or team responsible for performing the task.

- **When (when it will be done):** sets the deadline or schedule for completing the task.

- **Where (where it will be done):** identifies the location where the task will be performed.

- **How (how it will be done):** describes the methods and processes that will be used to perform the task.

- **How much (how much it will cost):** defines the cost or investment required to perform the task.

To use the 5W2H action plan, follow these steps:

- Identify what needs to be done and why.

- Define who will be responsible for performing the task.

- Establish when the task should be completed.

- Identify where the task will be performed.

- Define how the task will be performed.

- Estimate how much it will cost to perform the task.

- Check if the action plan is clear, complete, and consistent.

If you tend to want to see a big change in a few days, remember that working on your Personal Brand is like building a construction. It takes time for people to notice your positioning and for you to start reaping the rewards of your visibility. The biggest risk you run by letting anxiety take over is getting frustrated and giving up. Our suggestion: follow your action plan and celebrate small victories.

Lastly, the third pillar to the success of your Personal Brand is the courage to act. Courage to identify your values, courage to experience this journey of discovering your talents and goals. Courage to express yourself and position yourself clearly and coherently.

Courage to differentiate yourself and take risks. Without courage, we become stagnant, limited, and dependent on others. It's as if we hand our Personal Brand over to someone else and let them interpret it on their own. Therefore, this is a necessary virtue for anyone who wants to stand out and achieve new heights in life, as it makes you live in constant movement and growth. It encourages you to step out of your comfort zone and face the challenges and obstacles that will inevitably arise. Only with courage will we be protagonists.

" COURAGE TO DIFFERENTIATE YOURSELF AND TAKE RISKS. WITHOUT COURAGE, WE BECOME STAGNANT, LIMITED, AND DEPENDENT ON OTHERS. [...] ONLY WITH COURAGE WILL WE BE PROTAGONISTS."

Connecting the strength of professionals to the brand they are part of, within a strong and well-established company in the international logistics market like Craft, might seem like a simple task. After all, we thrive on services and the quality of our people, and our success story already proves what we are capable of.

But it's not.

As we navigated through the dynamics and conversations, I realized the importance of the method and the way it helps us see beyond where we are and who we are. It is a deep, intense, and surprisingly revealing and inspiring exercise. Observing the dance of well-placed words and well-observed insights at every connection made me certain that I was witnessing a true art of recognizing our strengths and guiding our thoughts and voices toward them.

This process revealed to us a universe of possibilities and potential capable of generating the sense of direction and spark in our eyes that every high-performing executive seeks.

In a transformational journey, where our greatest mission is to cultivate organizational change and drive new growth, finding the best in our people aligned with the best of our brand not only accelerated our progress but also allowed us to dream again.

Priscilla Bueno,
CTO - Chief Transformation Officer, Board Member - CRAFT GROUP

CHAPTER 12

LIVE IN BETA AND FLY

About seven years ago, when we began to explore the concept of Personal Branding, the topic was still little known in Brazil. The topic captivated us because it summarized many of the experiences we had intuitively experienced in our executive and consulting careers. At that time, we were noticing an increase in individual protagonism and the awareness of our ability to provide value to the world through our unique characteristics. Furthermore, the search for fulfillment and happiness in work as our true selves, without having to create a persona, was and continues to be on the rise. We did not imagine the extent this work would gain, nor that so many people would be interested in what we had to offer. It has been gratifying to exchange with so many professionals who teach us by entrusting us with their life stories, career challenges, and aspirations.

This book does not claim to be a definitive guide on the subject of Personal Branding, because this topic is far from being complete. Like all new subjects, it brings restlessness. There is still much to be explored, and we are honored to be part of this collective journey, with many other professionals who have dedicated themselves to the subject. Personal Branding, as we work on it, focused on Identity, starts from the principle that each person is unique. In each journey we start, we learn something new . There is nothing more beautiful than this incompleteness: knowing that there is more to be discovered. We suggest that you also find beauty in this constant discovery and not put pressure on yourself to define an immutable and definitive Personal Brand. Allow yourself to use all your knowledge to take action and dance through your cycles with awareness, reinventing yourself whenever life challenges you or presents new possibilities.

BetaFLY was born from our belief that every human being is constantly in " Beta." "Beta version" is a term used in technology to indicate a preliminary version of software that is still in development but is already at a stage sufficient to be launched on the market, even though it may need some adjustments. These adjustments happen as users use the software and point out improvements. "Living in Beta" is a great way to approach life because it indicates that we are constantly evolving.

The FLY® Method is not just a way for both of us, Giuliana and Susana, to put our purpose into action by combining our individual talents. This method has a beginning, middle, and end - but your Personal Brand does not. It continues to renew, in constant "beta." So, always revisit the steps of this method. As Adam Grant, whom we have mentioned several times in this book, said, "It takes confident humility to admit that we are a work in progress." It takes humility to acknowledge that we are always a work in progress.

The concept of "living in FLY," which means "flying" in English, is also very symbolic because it indicates courage and determination to achieve goals that we may not always imagine we could conquer in our lives. We are moving towards our goals and willing to take risks, facing necessary challenges. The important thing is to be willing to adjust our course in flight, as it is only in motion that we can perceive the necessary adjustments to reach the final goal. The concept of the "BetaFly" brand, which combines living in "beta" and "flying," represents the most valuable thing that the FLY® Method can deliver to each person who has the opportunity to experience this journey with us.

"BetaFLY" sounds similar to the word "butterfly" in English, which evokes the image of transformation and the metamorphosis of a caterpillar. This is a beautiful metaphor that we like to associate with our FLY® Method – just like a caterpillar goes through a transformation process to become a butterfly, we also go through different phases in our lives and can emerge and bring to the surface, to our consciousness, what is most valuable to transform into our best version, into what we are meant to be uniquely and singularly. This quest will lead you to expand your consciousness and also expand to the people you relate to. Put yourself in motion, allow yourself to flow with life, and be who you were born to be.

Live in Beta, and Fly.

WHAT OUR
PARTNERS SAY

I dedicate this text to Susana Arbex, from BetaFly, an incredible professional and an admirable person. Her ability to balance a vibrant professional life with being a dedicated mother is truly inspiring. Furthermore, she is open to opinions and suggestions and possesses an amazing sense of friendship.

In this era where social media has become a driving force in enhancing executive careers, the strengthening of personal branding is increasingly important—and this is where Susana shines. Her pursuit of knowledge through postgraduate studies and courses abroad has brought valuable experience to the BetaFly method, which transforms names into powerful brands, with deep reflections on careers and purpose.

I highly recommend the work of the duo Susana Arbex and Giuliana Tranquilini, who have elevated the image of executives in both Brazil and abroad. Their international journey is impressive, and their work comes highly recommended.

Susana, your journey and skills are truly inspiring. Thank you for your dedication and for being a source of inspiration to so many people. I wish you continuous success on both your professional and personal journeys.

Adriano Bravo
Founder & CEO - Petra Group

Susana, I'll share two perspectives: one as the coordinator of the postgraduate program, reflecting on the impact of your course within the curriculum, and the other based on feedback I received from the students.

What I found so valuable was that the Personal Branding course was placed at the end of the Branding postgraduate program, making it a sort of "meta-lesson"—an invitation for students to reflect on themselves at the conclusion of the course.

The way you built the course was fascinating, showing sensitivity and a deep understanding of the difference between developing a brand for a company and developing a personal brand. It's a socio-emotional development process, recognizing points of tension and managing them gently in a way that enhances potential.

Students leave your course with a better-organized sense of their Personal Brand and, at the same time, with a heightened sensitivity and awareness of the importance of empathy and listening—something your course conveys naturally and powerfully.

The students describe your class as "a breath of fresh air." They felt they had gained significant knowledge. While the process wasn't always easy, it was profoundly enriching. Your gentle approach allowed students to embrace their own vulnerabilities, leaving them feeling more open and confident in expressing themselves.

Ana Cotta
Coordinator of the Branding Postgraduate Program - IED Rio

Imagine the following situation: you have spent years honing your skills, acquiring knowledge, and perfecting your practice. You are an exceptional professional! But there are many others with similar specialties, characteristics, and qualities. So, how do you stand out among so many options? How do you become a reference in your field? The answer lies in branding!

Giuliana and Susana show you the path in this comprehensive book!

Brand management is essential for anyone who wants to build a solid and lasting reputation in the market.

Branding doesn't apply only to companies or products but also to individuals! The authors of this book explain how to create a unique identity that represents who you are, what you believe in, and the value you can bring.

Your brand is a reflection of your expertise, your approach, and the experience people can expect when they choose you as a professional.

A strong brand helps establish trust and credibility from the start.

Building a Personal Brand involves several key elements that will define how you are perceived by people and the market in general.

Giuliana and Susana provide details on how to define your professional identity and reflect on your values, mission, and the purpose that drives you.

What are the characteristics and attributes that best represent who you are as a professional?

"Your Personal Brand" is an assertive and effective work to help you build your identity. Reading this book will make a significant difference in your professional life.

Happy reading!

Christiane Pelajo
Journalist, communicator, and speaker

When it comes to careers, why is it so hard to talk about ourselves rather than just our work? Behind every professional, there is an individual, and it's undeniable that everyone has a Personal Brand. It's a concept that goes beyond résumés and achievements—it is the authentic expression of who we are and the value we bring to the world. However, for many professionals, uncovering and strengthening their Personal Brand can be a major challenge.

It is with great pleasure and immense pride in my friends that I present to you this book by Giuliana and Susana, two extraordinary executives who have fully immersed themselves in this fascinating field and developed a unique methodology. The FLY® Method demystifies concepts and encourages us to reflect on how we can make an impact through our truth. With an inspiring journey, they have guided professionals on a path of self-discovery, freeing them from masks and constraints so they can reach their full potential.

By delving into the core principles of an authentic Personal Brand, Giuliana and Susana open a world of possibilities for all readers. They invite us to discover our strengths and develop a voice that echoes our inner truth. Through their skillful and powerful words, and with real and inspiring examples, they show us how we can stand out in our careers while living our purpose.

This book is a transformative read—one that could be the turning point you've been searching for in your career. As you turn these pages, be prepared to challenge yourself, to question ingrained beliefs, and to embrace the true essence of who you are. Giuliana and Susana are generous and authentic guides, and their knowledge and passion resonate in every chapter. Immerse yourself in moving stories, practical advice, and profound insights that will help you discover the transformative power of your own voice.

May this book be the catalyst that leads you to a bright future where your Personal Brand stands out, and your impact is undeniable.

Enjoy your reading!

Daniela Cachich,
President of Beyond Beer at Ambev and Board Member of Grupo Boticário

---

Our partnership began in 2018, when I received a message from Giuliana (still based in Brazil at the time). She was transitioning from the corporate world into Personal Branding and moving from Brazil to the U.S.. Our connection was immediate. She shared her journey with major Brazilian brands and companies in the field of branding, expressing her desire to work with Personal Branding and sought my guidance for the process.

From the beginning, she expressed her interest in Personal Branding, and I remember her asking if there would be a conflict of interest (I believe this was a concern at the time). Her authenticity and honesty were always captivating. Of course, I embarked on this journey with her using our MétodoYOU®, which we've successfully used to support professionals worldwide—from the USA to Japan—who want to develop their expertise in Personal Branding.

Years later, I invited her to speak at the PBEX Experience® 2022, an international event on Personal Branding that brings together experts from around the world. Giuliana's dedication and work have positioned her more firmly in this borderless market, from Silicon Valley to the world.

We are all part of building this narrative, and BetaFly plays an essential role in it. I am proud of Giuliana's journey and excited about what lies ahead. I wish her continued success, impact, and purpose in the world of Personal Branding.

Daniela Viek

Co-Founder - Youbrand.Company, International Specialist in Personal Branding

---

In a connected world, how professionals position themselves in the market, especially in the digital space, is crucial.

In one of my MBA classes, I had the honor of hosting Susana Arbex from BetaFly as a guest speaker. She presented the FLY® Method and spoke to executives about the importance of developing their Personal Brands to enhance both online presence and professional visibility overall.

The students not only gained insights into Personal Branding but also connected it to corporate brand strategies, which provided significant value to all participants.

Farah Diba Braga

Ph.D. and Marketing Professor - Insper

As a partner, I've witnessed the maturity the method has achieved, continuously evolving and integrating new knowledge. It's gratifying to observe the transformation of clients—not because they conform to a pre-set standard, but because they embrace their true selves.

This is the beauty of the method: it is built entirely on valuing authenticity. It helps individuals identify their strengths and, by communicating them effectively and intentionally, unlocks new opportunities along their desired path.

Flávia Lima
Career Coach for Women and Trainer in Behavioral Skills

I had the opportunity to meet Giuliana during a workshop I teach at Stanford Continuing Studies, where I have been an instructor for over 17 years. On that occasion, the topic was Nonverbal Communication.

In our highly connected society, the image we project and the way we communicate play a fundamental role in personal and professional success. Personal Branding is the essence of who we are and what we represent.

It distinguishes us in an increasingly competitive world, allowing us to be recognized and valued for our skills, expertise, and authenticity.

Nonverbal communication, in turn, is a powerful tool that complements verbal expression and conveys subtle yet impactful messages that can reinforce or weaken the verbal message. Gestures, posture, facial expressions, and even the way we use space around us influence how others perceive us.

Mastering this silent language enables us to project confidence, credibility, and competence, creating stronger connections with our target audience.

Giuliana, as a Personal Branding expert, is constantly expanding her knowledge in this field, and nonverbal communication is essential for expressing any Personal Brand. I wish you much success with your book, and may you continue to impact many clients with your work!

Jeff Cabili
Instructor - Stanford Continuing Studies

I witnessed the birth of BetaFly and have been a fan of the innovative work led by Susana and Giuliana.

With extensive knowledge, experience, competence, and originality, they created the FLY® Method, which takes us on a guided journey of deep self-discovery, breaking paradigms and limiting beliefs. Through their guidance, I learned to bring awareness, intentionality, planning, and discipline to something I had always done intuitively: building my Personal Brand, my greatest asset.

I also learned that I am always a work in progress and need to repeatedly ask myself: What have I not yet shown the world? What is holding me back from working on my Personal Brand? What is my unique value proposition? What problem do I solve?

Personal Branding is about connection and trust. When we put our brand into action, we tell the world, courageously and authentically, how we create value through our identity. This is a unique, personal, and non-transferable process.

Neivia Justa
Journalist and Corporate Activist Leader - Founder of #JustaCausa

---

Discussing the importance of Personal Branding in medical career development is not just necessary—it's a strategic vision. It serves as the foundation for building a solid and assertive career.

In my experience recommending Giu's work to doctors, I can confidently say that the results have been remarkable. I've witnessed true transformations in self-awareness and in recognizing unique strengths within each professional, leading to better positioning and a clearer definition of their target audience.

Congratulations, Giu, for living your mission of helping so many people find their place in the world with clarity and ease.

Silvane Castro
CEO - Seven Gestão Consultoria

REFERENCES

Burt, Ronald Stuart. "Structural Holes and Good Ideas." *American Journal of Sociology* 110, no. 2 (September 2004): 349–399. Accessed June 20, 2023. https://www.bebr.ufl.edu/sites/default/files/Burt%20-%20 2004%20-%20Structural%20Holes%20and%20Good%20Ideas.pdf.

Cain, Susan. *Quiet: The Power of Introverts in a World That Can't Stop Talking.* Translated by Ana Carolina Bento Ribeiro. Rio de Janeiro: HarperCollins Brasil, 2017.

Campbell, Joseph. *The Hero with a Thousand Faces.* São Paulo: Pensamento, 1989.

Carvalho, Maytê. *Persuasion: How to Use Rhetoric and Persuasive Communication in Your Personal and Professional Life.* Buzz Editora, 2020.

Cialdini, Robert, Ph.D. *Influence, New and Expanded: The Psychology of Persuasion.* 2nd ed. Rio de Janeiro: HarperCollins Brasil, 2021.

Clear, James. *Atomic Habits: An Easy and Proven Way to Build Good Habits and Break Bad Ones.* Rio de Janeiro: Alta Life, 2019.

Clifton, Donald O., Ph.D. *StrengthsFinder.* 1st ed. São Paulo: Sextante, 2019.

CliftonStrengths. Accessed June 20, 2023. https://www.gallup.com/Cliftonstrengths/Pt/Home.aspx.

Csikszentmihalyi, Mihaly. *Flow: The Psychology of Optimal Experience*. New York: HarperCollins, 2008.

"DNA Structure and Function." Khan Academy. Accessed June 20, 2023. https://www.khanacademy.org/test-prep/mcat/biomolecules/dna/a/dna-structure-and-function.

De Smet, Aron, Bonnie Dowling, Bryan Hancock, and Bill Schaninger. "The Great Attrition is Making Hiring Harder. Are You Searching the Right Talent Pools?" *McKinsey & Company*, July 13, 2022. Accessed June 20, 2023. https://www.mckinsey.com/capabilities/people-and-organizational-performance/our-insights/the-great-attrition-is-making-hiring-harder-are-you-searching-the-right-talent-pools.

Dubar, Claude. *Socialization: The Construction of Social and Professional Identities*. Translated by Andréa S. M. Silva. São Paulo: Martins Fontes, 2020.

Durkheim, Émile. *The Division of Labor in Society*. São Paulo: Martins Fontes, 1999.

Fishbach, Ayelet. *Get It Done: Surprising Lessons from the Science of Motivation*. New York: Little, Brown Spark, 2022.

Galloway, Scott. "The Algebra of Wealth." *Profgalloway.com*, 2022. Accessed June 20, 2023. https://www.profgalloway.com/the-algebra-of-wealth-2/.

Giddens, Anthony. *Modernity and Self-Identity*. Rio de Janeiro: Zahar, 2002.

Goleman, Daniel. *Emotional Intelligence: Why It Can Matter More Than IQ*. Rio de Janeiro: Objetiva, 1996.

Grant, Adam. *Give and Take: A Revolutionary Approach to Success*. Rio de Janeiro: Sextante, 2014.

Kapferer, Jean-Noel. *The New Strategic Brand Management: Creating and Sustaining Brand Equity Long Term.* 4th ed. London: Kogan Page, 2008.

Kaufmann, Jean-Claude. *The Invention of the Self: A Theory of Identity.* Lisbon: Instituto Piaget, 2004.

Lowery, Brian. *Selfless: The Social Creation of 'You'.* New York: Harper, 2023.

Martino, Luis Mauro de Sá. *Communication Theory: Ideas, Concepts, and Methods.* Rio de Janeiro: Vozes, 2014.

Mayew, William J., Christopher A. Parsons, and Mohan Venkatachalam. "Voice Pitch and the Labor Market Success of Male Chief Executive Officers." *Elsevier Science Direct.* Accessed June 20, 2023. https://www.sciencedirect.com/science/article/abs/pii/S1090513813000238.

Mehrabian, Albert. *Silent Messages: Implicit Communication of Emotions and Attitudes.* Belmont, CA: Wadsworth Publishing Company, 1972.

Merzenich, Michael, Ph.D. *Soft-Wired: How the New Science of Brain Plasticity Can Change Your Life.* Parnassus, 2013.

Monarth, Harrison. *Executive Presence, Second Edition: The Art of Commanding Respect Like a CEO.* New York: McGraw-Hill, 2019.

Peters, Tom. "The Brand Called You." *Fast Company*, October 1997.

Peters, Tom. *The Brand You 50 (Reinventing Work): Fifty Ways to Transform Yourself from an "Employee" into a Brand That Shouts Distinction, Commitment, and Passion! (Reinventing Work Series).* New York: Knopf, 1999.

Rea, Shilo. "Carnegie Mellon Brain Imaging Research Shows How Unconscious Processing Improves Decision-Making." *Carnegie Mellon University*, February 13, 2013. Accessed June 20, 2023. https://www.cmu.edu/news/stories/archives/2013/february/feb13_unconsciousthought.html.

Ries, Al, and Jack Trout. *Positioning: The Battle for Your Mind: How to Be Seen and Heard in the Overcrowded Marketplace.* New York: McGraw-Hill, 2001.

Saint-Exupéry, Antoine de. *The Little Prince.* 1st ed. Belo Horizonte: Garnier, 2022.

Simon, Carmen. *Impossible to Ignore: How to Influence Your Audience's Memory and Spark Action Using Brain Science.* New York: McGraw-Hill Education, 2016.

Wickre, Karen. *Taking the Work Out of Networking: An Introvert's Guide to Making Connections That Count.* New York: Gallery Books, 2018.

Zanatta, Mariana Scussel. "In the Webs of Identity." Accessed August 16, 2023. https://www.uricer.edu.br/site/pdfs/perspectiva/132_232.pdf.

ABOUT THE AUTHORS

GIULIANA TRANQUILINI

With over 25 years of executive experience at top organizations like Havaianas, Natura, AlmapBBDO, and Spencer Stuart, Giuliana Tranquilini is a seasoned marketing and branding expert. As the founder of BetaFly, she has developed a unique methodology to help individuals build powerful Personal Brands. A sought-after speaker and mentor, she is one of the authors of the best-selling book *Rise and Raise Others*. With degrees from ESPM and certifications in coaching and Personal Branding, she has further honed her skills through programs at IDEO, Stanford, and Northwestern Kellogg focusing on storytelling, communication, influence, and data-driven digital marketing strategies.

SUSANA ARBEX

Susana Arbex holds 28 years of executive experience in Marketing, Branding, and Strategic Planning. She has worked in renowned companies such as Natura, Santander, and T4F. As a consultant, she led branding projects for Klabin, Brastemp, Raízen, Cacau Show, BTG Investimentos, BRF, and Pepsico. Currently, she serves as a Consultant, Speaker, Advisor, and Professor. Ms. Araujo holds a specialization in Marketing and Leadership from Fundação Getúlio Vargas (FGV), an Executive MBA from Fundação Dom Cabral, a post-MBA from the Kellogg School of Management, and has completed leadership and executive presence programs at Wharton, Cornell, and INSEAD.

Giuliana and Susana are Personal Branding specialists with triple certification from Reach CC USA and co-founders of Betafly Brandmakers, with offices in São Paulo and Palo Alto.

BETAFLY
BRANDMAKERS

www.ingramcontent.com/pod-product-compliance
Lightning Source LLC
Chambersburg PA
CBHW022112210326
41597CB00047B/254